YOUR I

MW01292770

101 Great Ideas to Simplify Your Life

How to Slash Stress, Ditch the Drama and Intensify Your Tranquility

MICHAEL E. ANGIER

Published by Success Networks International, Inc.
Tampa Bay, Florida 34609-9509
www.SuccessNet.org

ISBN: 9781700281340

Reviews

"Michael, you have nailed this one! I absolutely loved '101 Great Ideas to Simplify Your Life'. *After reading the whole book, I have decided it's too good to put on the shelf. I'm going to read it again, but this time focusing on and implementing just one tip per day. I'm sure this is going to be a runaway best seller."*

—Allyn Cutts
www.CuttsGroup.com

"Michael Angier's book, '101 Great Ideas to Simplify Your Life,' *improved my life in one day. Disorder, confusion and chaos were booted out. Order and peace arrived. It blew my mind with its simplicity and good sense. I discovered actions I had never before considered. I read it in the morning. By afternoon, I dumped 3 habits and felt better about myself. This book could easily be titled,* 'The Zen of Serene Living.'"

—Burt Dubin, president,
Personal Achievement Institute

"Brilliant book. Each nugget of wisdom in this book is practical and immediately useful. Michael Angier shows you that a simple life is really a rich and rewarding life. The value contained in these pages is priceless. You'll want to read this book over and over again."

—Debbie Bermont,
www.OutrageousBusinessGrowth.com

"I have read every book Michael Angier has written in the last few years. I enjoyed them all. But '101 Great Ideas to Simplify Your Life' touched me like none of the others. From it, I learned some simple adjustments I can make to better organize my life.

In this book Michael helped me identify my vision of a simple life and then provided simple suggestions to help me realize that vision. This book is filled with action points and resources to help you fill your life with beauty and simplicity."

—David DeFord
www.OrdinaryPeopleCanWin.com

"I want to simplify my life. That makes me part of a growing demographic of individuals who are tired of the 'bigger, better, more' consumer model of living. Of all the books on living simply that I've seen, this is one of the most straightforward, practical and useful. Advice for simplicity in the real world from real people—advice that actually works—in one book that I can pick up and open to any page for great ideas. This new addition to Michael Angier's '101 Great Ideas' library is a winner!"

—Rick Frishman, president,
co-author of AUTHOR 101 series of books
www.Author101.com

"If simplicity is more than just a buzz-phrase to you; if a simpler life is more than just a passing phase to you, then you need this book. When I first heard of the concept, I was intrigued: survey thousands of people for their best ideas, tips and advice on how to simplify life and publish their responses in a book. Now that I've read it, I'm even more impressed. Organized into relevant categories, these 101 ideas are very practical words of wisdom. By implementing even a small percentage of these ideas, my life will transform . . . Simply!"

—Dr. Philip Humbert
author, speaker, personal success coach
www.PhilipHumbert.com

"Simplify. Simplify. Simplify. In this overcomplicated world we live in, we must find ways to lead simpler lives in order to make room to move forward. Your excellent book, '101 Great Ideas to Simplify Your Life,' hits the nail squarely on the head, with practical and actionable advice that will indeed simplify and greatly improve your life. I especially like your 'one year rule.' Having just experienced a severe 'closet cleaning,' I felt the freedom that just this one action brought. Michael's book provides plenty more great ideas that I need to implement. I wholeheartedly recommend this as a must-read for everyone."

—Rick Beneteau
award-winning author and host of the Mentor Message Podcasts www.MentorAudio.com

"A Lifesaver! If you've 'had it' and are ready for a simpler life, this book is for you! Best Life Architect Michael Angier shows you how to 'file it, finish it, or forget it.' Not only does he reveal how to declutter any "gunk" that is complicating your life, but you also learn how to keep it that way! If you only buy one book on simplifying your life, make it this one!"

—Kristie Tamsevicius
author of *I Love My Life: A Mom's Guide to Working from Home*
www.Webmomz.com

"I love this book! I love it so much, I was going to write a similar book myself—that's how vital I believe the subject of simplifying your life is. It is at the core of finding peace, happiness and balance. And now you have done me a great favor—you have saved me the time of writing the book myself! So thank you on behalf of all of my subscribers who I know will reap a lifetime of benefits from your beautifully compiled book. And thank you for putting into words the many suggestions I never even thought of—which I will now use to further simplify my own life!"

—Dr. Michael Norwood
best-selling author of *The 9 Insights of the Wealthy Soul*
www.WealthySoul.com

"Several months ago I put a big yellow sticky note on one of my kitchen cabinets. I had a single question on it: 'How can I make my life simpler?'

I put it there to focus my attention on that one thought because life was getting much too complicated. There's so much input these days—glorious when you want it, a nightmare when you don't.

Every time I went into the kitchen and looked at the note, my brain went searching for an answer. But just as quickly, there would be something that needed my attention and off I went.

And then—like a wonder of wonders—Michael and Dawn Angier invite me to review Michael's latest book 101 Great Ideas to Simplify Your Life. *After I stopped laughing at the odd coincidence, I simply approached Michael's work with gratitude. He's written a book that fits perfectly into my life right now— and yours—if you're a busy professional like me. I can read any one page and get a solution I can use to lighten up my life.*

I simply say 'Thank you, thank you' to all the wonderful people who contributed to Michael's new book—and to Michael—for writing such a meaningful piece of work. Thanks for giving me a very handy tool, just at the right time.

—JoAnna Brandi
publisher and Customer Care Coach®
president of JoAnna Brandi & Company, Inc

> *"Our life is frittered away by detail . . .*
> *simplify, simplify, simplify."*
> —Henry David Thoreau

It's reported that Ralph Waldo Emerson commented on Henry David Thoreau's quote with: "Seems as though one simplify would have been enough."

Table of Contents

Foreword by Frank Lunn

Earl Nightingale observed: "If you look at what everybody else is doing and do the exact opposite, you may never make another mistake as long as you live." Our world is moving faster and faster and even the concept of simplifying our lives is counter-intuitive. Our world is progress. We are moving at a pace continuing to ratchet up, making our lives ever more complex—even in the promise of increased technology supposedly designed to make our lives easier.

We evolve, adapt and upgrade to keep up with "everybody." This is a trap. Instead of blindly following the path of progress, it's time for a much-needed change in perspective and a pause to readjust our bearing.

I was in this harried, fast-paced moment when I sat down to write this foreword for Michael's *101 Great Ideas to Simplify Your Life*. I began reading the material and was immediately captivated and pulled in. I couldn't put it down. This book spoke directly to my needs, as a guide for changes in my own life.

As an entrepreneur for more than ten years, I've been truly blessed to lead a fantastic team while growing a multi-million dollar group of companies. And along the way, I've discovered additional opportunities to share my entrepreneurial passions as an author of three books and as a speaker.

I have years of practical experience. And I feel secure in my abilities and knowledge in personal development, marketing and leadership. I am confident in my abilities of being a visionary, able to assess and develop opportunities in the future. None of this is meant to be prideful—only to put what I'm about to say in context.

I feel competent and confident in all of the above. But I must admit in complete candor, what I struggle with more than just about anything is (gulp)—simplicity.

If I was paranoid, I would think my good friend Michael (in cahoots with my wife, closest friends and business associates) wrote this book specifically for me, as some kind of intervention. I imagine you'll feel the same as you read on. Michael's practical insights and action plans reveal the deep-seated challenges we each face in order to keep our lives from spinning wildly out of control.

Simplicity and simplifying our lives is not easy as we fight against the current of our lives. The deep desire to gain balance in our lives makes us want to fight complexity with more complexity as we look for additional technology through hardware and software programs, gadgets and gizmos.

Yes, this hits me at the core, because my natural tendency is to add to and complicate things. Fortunately, I was able to immediately take action on some of Michael's ideas. And I've already seen benefits. For me, this will be a work in progress to slow down, simplify and ask better questions of myself before, during and after I take something on.

As you read and take action on the ideas in *101 Great Ideas to Simplify Your Life,* you'll find it simple in construction and very easy to follow. This is a book of practical wisdom and potent insights.

I am proud to know Michael Angier and call him friend. He is a person of deep knowledge, vast experience and great character, devoted to achieving his victories and his values through the service he provides to and through others.

Michael E. Angier

Enjoy and apply *101 Great Ideas to Simplify Your Life*. You will most certainly improve the quality of your life and the quality of your relationships.

—Frank F. Lunn
Best-selling author of *Carpe Aqualis! "Seize the Wave"*
www.KahunaPower.com

Introduction

The world we live in is very complex. There's a delicate harmony between our inner lives: dreams, hopes, doubts and uncertainties and our outer lives: tasks, people, politics and events. It's no wonder that the trend toward conscious simplicity continues to gain momentum.

Do you crave more simplicity? Are dreams of a simpler life taking hold? Then you're part of a growing demographic of individuals who want to take the dream one step further. The fact that you're reading this means you've made a conscious decision to create a simpler path for yourself. Congratulations.

This book is for anyone on a quest for more simplicity. It was born from the ideas and comments of hundreds of individuals who wanted to share and explore the concept. We published it because we believe in the possibilities of voluntary simplicity and want to participate in the movement. This book is for you, for your loved ones and for your future generations. We hope it helps you leave a legacy.

Why Simplify?

Living simply looks different to each person. Your personal version of simplicity is not like anyone else's. There's no blueprint for creating it. Consider it more like a masterpiece that only your unique experiences, circumstances and talents can create. Everyone's simplicity looks different. It's a good idea to start developing a clear picture of your simple life. But first, let's look at some possible reasons for making it happen:

Think about why you want it. What reasons are most important to you? Your reasons for making change become your motivation. Keep your motivation in clear view while you're working toward simplicity.

Here are some possible reasons to simplify your life:

- You want more time for yourself

- Your family needs more time together

- You're tired of feeling overwhelmed

- You know there's more to life

- It seems like no matter how fast you run, you're not getting anywhere

What are your reasons?

What Does Simplicity Look Like to You?

If a simpler life is your goal, one of the first things you'll need (other than the desire to make it happen) is a clear vision of your desired outcome. Before you begin implementing the strategies we've listed in this book, take the time to develop your unique picture of a simple life. Spend some time considering how you want your life to look.

Here are some questions to help you develop your picture of simplicity:

In your simpler life . . .

. . . where do you live?

. . . what is your home like?

. . . what do you spend your days doing?

. . . what do you spend time doing with the people in your life?

. . . what chores do you no longer do?

. . . what worries no longer bother you?

. . . what "stuff" have you gotten rid of?

. . . what do you do a lot more of?

. . . how do you feel?

Remember, an integral step in developing your picture is picturing yourself already enjoying your goal. When creating your personal vision of simplicity, include yourself in the picture!

Organizing vs. Simplifying

Voluntary simplicity isn't an extra chore to add to your "to-do" list. Neither is it about getting organized (although that's part of it). Living simply is about letting go of things—ideas, activities, behaviors, items, relationships—that unnecessarily encumber the flow of your life. It's about giving yourself permission to breathe freely every day.

You've heard the adage "less is more"? Simplicity is a perfect example of this principle. With a simpler life, you'll be richer. You'll have more time, more energy, more peace and more space to become the individual you're meant to be.

Apart from all the esoteric benefits of choosing a simpler life, there are more down-to-earth, practical benefits, too. Imagine less clutter in your home, more time to do what you want. Experience better health, enriched relationships, less stress and a calmer demeanor.

We Surveyed—Our Readers Responded

The seed that grew into this book was a survey we conducted. We asked SuccessNet subscribers from all over the world, in every walk of life, to share their ideas, strategies and thoughts on simplicity.

We got a great response. People wanted to discuss the concept, wanted to explore the principles of simplicity and to share their ideas. Many of their survey responses are included in this book. You'll also find some interesting quotes from respondents.

Apart from collecting strategies for simple living, we also collected the following data:

Do you consider your life to be more complicated than you'd like it to be?

      Yes 76.58%

      No 23.42%

Do you have a significant desire to experience more simplicity in any area of your life?

      Yes 88.59%

      No 11.41%

Do you feel that achieving more simplicity is particularly difficult in today's world?

      Yes 77.51%

      No 22.49%

No surprise there. But the real question is *how* do you achieve more simplicity? The responses in this book made a lot of sense. None of them were earth-shattering; none of them will spark a revolution. But they do work.

You could implement one per month and take a decade to achieve your version of simplicity—or one strategy per week, for two years. But the best plan is to select the strategies that fit your life and to implement them until they're a seamless part of your daily life.

Just as no two people's pictures of simplicity will be the same, the combination of strategies that work for you will be unique. You may choose to read all the strategies and design your own. Or you may use certain ones as a template and tweak them to fit your circumstances. In any case, decide on the strategies that will work for you and implement them. Don't make simplicity overly complex; keep it simple!

How to Use the Categories

We organized the sage suggestions from our *"101 Great Ideas to Simplify Your Life"* into nine categories (chapters). This will make it easier for you to locate advice and dig deeper into the various subjects.

Chapter 1: Enough Stuff—Manage Your Material Things & Organize Your Stuff

The majority of the survey responses offered advice on simplifying our lives by reducing, managing and organizing all that *stuff* in our lives. For better or for worse, we live in a consumer society. It's interesting how consumer products are supposed to make our lives more convenient, more fun, easier, smarter and faster. Yet here we are harried to distraction. All too often, our once-desired consumer product quickly devolves into clutter once we bring it home. Clutter is an enemy of simplicity. It sucks your soul and robs you of rest, time and ease.

Chapter 2: Enough Time—Your Routines, Planning and Time Management

We're all familiar with the story: the advent of all the modern conveniences was supposed to give us more time for leisure and fewer hassles. Remember when the promise of computers was "a paperless office?" Well, one way or another, our lives are busier, more cluttered and more frenzied than ever.

There are 'only' 24 hours each day in which to juggle our health, our relationships, our duties and our rest. It's all too common to spend so much time attending to our duties and to the needs of others, that our own health and rest get the short shift (literally).

If there is one area of our lives where a modicum of planning and a simple system or two can make a world of difference, it's this area—time management. Simplify this area of your life and you'll experience significant change for the better.

Chapter 3: Money—Your Work and Your Income

It seems like a world without money would be the simplest of all. On the other hand, "enough" money for everyone would simplify things, too. One way or another, your money and how you earn and manage it are fundamental elements of your life and therefore an integral ingredient to your simplified life.

An old adage says that "money makes the world go 'round." Actually gravity makes the world go 'round, but money can make your head spin when you don't have a handle on it.

The following strategies will help to simplify your financial life so that your world doesn't need to revolve around it.

Chapter 4: What to Do—Add, Increase, Practice, Learn, Do

At first, it may seem a bit counterintuitive to *add* things to do in order to make things simpler. However, the key is to add behaviors and habits that ultimately *reduce* the complexity of your life, instead of just increasing the length of your to-do list.

Voluntary simplicity, of course, is more than a series of new strategies to try. It's a new way of being in the world. Once you've decided to simplify things, you'll add a new layer of innovative thoughts and behaviors to your day. Soon, with repetition and practice, these will become habits. And these habits will form the foundation of your new nature.

Chapter 5: What Not To Do—Avoid, Reduce, Stop, Let Go, Move On

If your hands are so full that your days are a juggling act, it's time to drop something. You just can't continue picking things up and adding them to your tasks. You need to know when and what to let go so that your life transforms into a simple one.

This chapter describes ideas for decreasing complexities in your life. It requires the ability and the willingness to stop, drop, and yes, even avoid certain things. These strategies will help you develop your "not-to-do list."

Chapter 6: Make the Connections—Your Relationships

The songs say that love makes the world go round, all you need is love and what the world needs now is love, love.

Unless you're living as a hermit on a remote mountainside (in which case your life is already quite simple!), your day is filled with human interactions. If you choose the path of a simpler life, you'll eventually need to address those connections. Relationships—the good, the bad and the weird—make up so much of our lives that they simply cannot be ignored. Here are some strategies offered by our survey participants that can help you simplify the relationships in your life.

Chapter 7: Alter Your Attitude—Your Focus

Your mental attitude is truly the source of so much of your experience of the world. How you are in the world dictates the world you live in. Cynics live in a cynical world; the frightened live in a hostile world; the doubtful live in an uncertain world. Fortunately, while we have very little influence over the world itself, we have absolute influence over our own attitudes. Remember, the merry live in a cheerful world; the compassionate live in a loving world; the adventuresome live in a thrilling world.

What kind of world do you live in?

Chapter 8: Be Balanced—Your Health & Well-Being

All of your possessions, relationships, hobbies and responsibilities—each and every one of them—are entirely dependent on the maintenance of your own health. Your to-do lists and clutter-busting strategies suddenly mean little if you're faced with a health crisis. Pay attention to how balanced your life is; your health depends on it. And so much depends on your health, doesn't it?

Chapter 9: Know Thyself—Your Self-Awareness

What could be simpler than knowing yourself? Well, as it turns out, virtually everything in life is simpler!

This final section of the book offers ideas for increasing your self-knowledge and awareness. These strategies, more than any others in the book, speak to the deeper aspects of your life. It's one thing to clear clutter from your junk drawer at the office, and another to clear your mind and become more of who you're meant to be.

Michael E. Angier

Chapter 1: Enough Stuff— Manage Your Material Things and Organize Your Stuff

The majority of the survey responses offered advice on simplifying our lives by reducing, managing and organizing all that stuff in our lives. For better or for worse, we live in a consumer society.

It's interesting how consumer products are supposed to make our lives more convenient, more fun, easier, smarter and faster. Yet here we are harried to distraction. All too often, our once-desired consumer product quickly devolves into clutter once we bring it home.

Clutter is an enemy of simplicity. It sucks your soul, robs you of rest, time and ease.

1. Clean out your closets every season.

This strategy appeared so many times in the survey that we placed it first. Yes, it is an extra chore; yes it'll take some time and planning. However, it really works. Whether you do it once, twice or more times per year, you'll notice a difference right away. Closets are places where we stuff the stuff we don't want to deal with. Often our tolerations are piled up in the closets. The saying goes: "out of sight out of mind." But it's never out of our consciousness. Tolerations create clutter in your mind.

2. Start using all the things that you've bought.

We've all done it: bought something really nifty, only to end up storing it and never (or hardly ever) using it. Maybe it's that bread machine or juicer in the kitchen cupboard. Or the jogging outfit in the closet. Maybe it's that once-shiny garden gadget gathering dust in the shed. Whatever it is, get it out and use it. If it turns out that it's not so helpful after all, give it away, sell it on eBay or otherwise recycle it.

The beauty of this strategy is in the indirect result. Next time you're wandering down the aisle of that big-box store in a consumer-daze, you'll think again about throwing that gadgetry gizmo in your shopping cart.

3. Develop systems for dealing with the piles of paper.

Whatever happened to the "paperless society" we were supposed to be living in after the advent of computers? These days, even my checkout receipt at the video store is big. Some stores even give me two pieces of paper, stapled together. There's more paper at work and at home. We have to have a system to deal with it. Here are some ideas suggested by our respondents:

In our community, we can leave a note for the post person not to leave junk mail in our box. (This survey respondent shared that they live in a rural community where they use post boxes.) So these days, all I get in the mail are letters and, of course, bills.

We purchased a paper shredder for about $20. Bank statements, paid bills, everything confidential, all get eaten by the shredder. Then we add them to our regular recycling.

Recycle. The more organized your home recycling depot is, the faster, cleaner and easier it is to maintain. Find a convenient space and set out several cardboard boxes (paper bags work, too) for each kind of recyclable.

At the office, it only takes about 10 minutes per month to cut up paper into note-sized pieces for jotting reminders or messages. Perfect for phone messages or note-taking.

Have a basket, drawer or shelf by the door for holding paper items that come in. Even better, have two baskets or drawers—one for incoming, one for outgoing.

4. Have few mechanical devices.

Oh, how we love our mechanical gadgets. If you're one of those people (you know who you are), you have a garage or shed filled with devices. The problem is that each device you own requires resources to keep it maintained. It takes money for replacing parts, for oil or gas, for a mechanic. It takes your time for figuring out what the problem is and fixing it or taking it to be fixed. It takes elbow grease to clean it and store it. Own only what you use. Rent seasonal equipment.

5. Stop accumulating things.

This is a top strategy. When it comes to buying, owning, storing, cleaning, maintaining, repairing and moving all that stuff, there is no way to simplify. One major key to simplicity is to simply stop accumulating things. Your closets won't fill up with dusty, unused things. You will never have to clean, fix or move something that you never needed in the first place. Maybe it takes a shift in your definition of the word "need." As in "I really need this extendable, multi-function, dual-textured toilet scrubber."

Of course, we don't know anyone who has completely escaped our consumer culture. Even the most down-shifted, simplicity-styled individuals accumulate some stuff. But the second part of this strategy is the brilliant part: "Anything not used for over a year must go!"

Remember, the specialty of this rule is that *anything* not used in over a year must go. That means clothes, shoes and kitchen gadgets, too.

6.   Keep only things that you can't live without.

There is always a "What If" for each and every piece of clutter you pick up to throw away. Remove the "What If" factor and just toss it. This is terrific when the clutter is still at the "Hmm, should I buy this?" stage. When you take a few moments to consider it before you even get to the checkout, you won't have to deal with the "What If" question. In the aisle of the store it's a nifty new gadget; at home, in the closet, it's just clutter.

7.   Replace the old with the new.

Whenever you buy something new, identify something similar that you can discard or give away.

We really like this simple strategy for simplifying. This technique will also help you at the store, during that moment when you decide whether or not to buy. No matter how thrilled you are with your shiny new purchase, you know you'll have to go home and find something to discard in order to maintain the balance.

8.   Make sure you use and love everything you own.

Still along the same lines of owning only items that you truly need and actually use, this strategy adds another element:

love. Even seemingly unlovable objects like a lawnmower can be loved, if you consider that it helps you create a beautiful backyard where you love to play with your kids. Or that old blanket of your grandmother's that you keep because you love snuggling up in it to watch movies.

Can you imagine what your life would be like if you loved everything in it? If you could walk around your home and set your eyes only on things that you really enjoyed and were grateful for? With an environment like that, anyone would feel more serene and blessed.

9.   Implement a 'one-touch' plan with papers.

Here's a strategy from a survey respondent that describes in detail a plan for dealing with paper clutter:

I sort out my mail at a spot where I have at arm's length my husband's desk chair (so he'll find it), my bill paying pile (so I don't lose it), and the waste basket (for obvious reasons). That way, I don't have to move any piles, and they don't get mixed in with each other. The 'one-touch' idea is a concept I picked up from a seminar a while back, which works with the thought that you waste time every time you touch something. So, to be more efficient, try to only touch it once. File it, do something with it or toss it.

Efficiency is a key principle in simplification. Don't make more work for yourself; make less. Figure out systems that help you to use the least amount of your time and energy to complete the task.

10. Everything needs a place.

This ranges from where you place your keys and cell phones when you enter your home (a high place, out of the reach of small hands), to wet towels (a low place so that small hands can use it). This goes for everything in the house, the garage, the tool shed, the attic and the basement. The anger, frustration and time that you save each morning as you and your family leave your home is worth its weight in gold.

11. Simplify the technology you use.

At times, because our world has become so busy and so consistently full, it seems that we spend more time tinkering with cell phones or new computer programs. Keep in mind the balance between setting up and programming those devices and actually enjoying the simplicity they promise.

12. Buy miniature or travel-size appliances.

For those appliances and gadgets that we need in our life, keep in mind that smaller items take up less space. For example, a travel iron folds and is easily packed in a suitcase. This way, you have one appliance for both home and travel.

A notebook computer generally has a higher price tag than a desktop computer and monitor, but it takes up a fraction of the space.

Consider travel hairdryers, smaller shavers, travel clocks and other smaller-sized appliances that can save you room in your home and give you more mobility.

13. Clean up your key ring.

Brilliant! How long would it take you to accomplish this? 5 minutes? Less? It's such a simple strategy, yet so effective. Many of us walk around with those "extra" keys on our key rings. It's a good chance there are keys on your key ring that you *never* use anymore; perhaps even keys that you can't remember what they're for. Keep those extra keys in a special drawer. Even better, label them first. Your key ring will only hold those keys that unlock things you use regularly.

"I empty my house, top to bottom. Only put back bare necessities and those things that reflect family and friendships that are so precious and fleeting. Give away everything that no longer fits, isn't played with or isn't needed and throw out the rest. Forget the video games, online time-wasters, and get back to basics. File it, finish it or forget it!"

—survey respondent

"Stand five minutes in front of your desk, drawers, garage, etc. and try looking at it through the eyes of an outsider. What do you see? Give or throw away everything that you do not expect to need in the near future. Fix, clean up and find places for those you do. Go through every corner of your house, company and life. I decided to do that. It has taken me three months now and will take two more. That's because it's not an easy task to do, but worth it from the first hour!"

—survey respondent

"Whenever I'm clothes shopping, I ask myself: do I absolutely love this? Do I love everything about it: color, material, fit?"

—survey respondent

"Simplifying my life means removing the clutter and junk that surrounds me. I have cleaned out every conceivable space in my house and given away a lot of items. I don't hold yard sales (not patient enough); I don't give to charities where I can't see how people benefit. I give things away to anyone who wants it. I put things out on my lawn with a huge FREE sign on it. It disappears."

—survey respondent

"We are cups, constantly and quietly being filled. The trick is knowing how to tip ourselves over and let the beautiful stuff out."

—Ray Bradbury

Websites

www.FlyLady.net

www.Shutterfly.com

www.RealSimple.com

www.eBay.com

www.SimpleLiving.net

Books

Let Go of Clutter by Harriet Schechter

One Thing at a Time: 100 Simple Ways to Live Clutter-Free Every Day by Cindy Glovinsky

The Secret to Being Fiercely Focused, by Michael Angier

Chapter 2:
Enough Time—Your Routines, Planning and Time Management

W e're all familiar with the story: the advent of all the modern conveniences was supposed to give us more time for
leisure and fewer hassles. Remember when the promise of computers was "a paperless office?" Well, one way or another, our lives are busier, more cluttered and more frenzied than ever.

There are 'only' 24 hours each day in which to juggle our health, our relationships, our duties and our rest. It's all too common to spend so much time attending to our duties and to the needs of others that our own health and rest get the short shift (literally).

If there is one area of our lives where a modicum of planning and a simple system or two can make a world of difference, it's this area—time management. Simplify this area of your life, and you'll experience significant change for the better.

14. Keep a routine for basic life tasks.
A basic routine will help you manage your day and all the different parts of it. At home, you can develop easy routines for getting ready in the mornings, for housework, for preparing meals, for sleeping. At work, you can develop routines for the end of your day, for answering calls and emails, for meetings, for filing paperwork.

Obviously, your routines must be flexible and adaptable. Otherwise, you just become a slave to the routine, and there's nothing good about that. Remember, the routines you develop are tools to help you, not extra duties to hinder you.

A simple outline of what needs to get done, who needs to do it and when it needs to happen will suffice. Write it down and post it. Or you can just develop a routine and allow it to become a habit.

Whatever way you choose to implement a routine into your life, you'll experience less hassles, less frustration, more calm and more time.

15. Reduce unwanted phone solicitation.

Answering a solicitation call can be a very frustrating time waster. When you answer an unwanted sales call, be sure to plainly (and politely) tell the caller to "please remove my name from your contact list." And be firm. You can discourage solicitation calls with a polite "No thank you" and then hang up.

Listening to the drone of an unwanted sales pitch is a drain on your energy. It's better to put it out of your life as quickly—and simply—as possible.

16. Maintain an errand list.

Keep a copy in your car, along with a box to hold items to be returned or repaired, etc. The time you spend dashing around running errands is something you can easily decrease, so that you'll have more time for things you want to do.

Errands force you to spend time in traffic, spend money, deal with bureaucracy and other tasks that aren't very enjoyable. Combine your errand-running on one afternoon per week.

Designate a spot in your home where you keep the items you'll need on your errands, as well as lists that you can add to throughout the week. Some of the benefits of this strategy include: saving on gas and driving time, keeping your schedule free for other things the rest of the week, feeling organized and more relaxed.

17. Write things that have to be done on paper.

With a paper list, you'll always have it with you and you won't have to log on to your computer to see your task list.

With an electronic task list, the likely probability is that you don't look at it. When something is written down on paper, you'll always have it with you.

18. If you have kids, limit their activities.

This way they have time to play, and you can have some family time. They don't need to be on the run every night. Over-scheduling family activities has become enough of an issue that health practitioners and teachers are publicly voicing their concerns.

Yes, routines and schedules can be very positive for adults and children alike, but children, especially, require down time. Think back to your own childhood. You have some very fine memories of just hanging out, playing times.

Give your kids the gift of doing-nothing time. Break them free of the never-ending schedules of activities.

19. Keep some time free or deliberately unplanned.

You can just do nothing. While basic routines will help you simplify your life by freeing up more time, it's what you choose to do with that "extra" time that'll make the difference to the quality of your life. Don't just fill up that time with more stuff to do. Do nothing!

If it's been a while since you've allowed yourself a period of time to just do nothing, you may have forgotten how wonderful it is. If you're out of practice, it may be difficult for you. You might feel compelled to turn on the TV, call someone or do some chores. Try not to. Do nothing on your own or do nothing with someone you like.

20. Deal with things as they come up.

For some people, the maxim "why do today what I can put off till tomorrow" is a way of life. And if you can live by this principle and function effectively in the world, with a minimum of distress, then all the power to you.

For many, however, procrastination packs a powerful punch: guilt, worry and stress. That's why we suggest that for a simplified life, it's usually best to attend to things as they come up.

And there are several ways you can deal with things without complicating your life. You can successfully defer or delegate a task in an organized manner so you won't end up "dropping the ball."

Make a couple of quick decisions about the task based on urgency and implementation. Then either do it, defer it or delegate and move on.

21. Stay home on your days off.

Many people are trapped on a treadmill of working to live. You work hard at a job all week, while dreaming of those days off. However, your days off are usually filled with obligations from all the other important segments of your life, like social, familial, household and community tasks.

What about time for you, without driving, without buying, without doing (much)? Plan to stay at home on a day off. Put it on your calendar.

Choose to putter, to pursue your hobby, to bake cookies, to read or to just hang around.

22. Prioritize your day's journey.

Plan out mentally the objectives of the day ahead. Each morning, take a few minutes to decide what you wish to accomplish by bedtime.

Rather than long "to-do" lists, formulate an idea of what's important for you to accomplish today; which priorities you want most to address. A few minutes at the start of your day can make a big difference to how you feel at the end of it.

23. Re-arrange your work hours.

Negotiate to arrange your work hours so that you start earlier. This one strategy could be the difference between starting your day maneuvering around busy traffic or breezing in on "roads less traveled."

Arrange your work hours so that you avoid the commuting crowds and give yourself more daylight hours off work. The added bonus is that your earlier schedule will give you a window of time to do your banking or other errands before these businesses close for the day.

24. Stop spending time to save money.

Value your time. Don't drive those extra miles to save a few cents on a grocery item. It's not worth your time. And consider hiring someone to do the chores you don't want to do.

One survey respondent had this perspective: if you can earn $50 per hour in your business, pay someone $25 per hour to clean your house. Think about ways you can spend money to save time.

25. Plan your menus ahead of time.

Planning meals—buying ingredients, preparing, cooking, serving the food several times a day—day after day, takes up a lot of time and energy. The more systemized you are in this area, the easier, quicker and more enjoyable it will become.

Menu planning is one of those things that really works to simplify our lives and yet, until it becomes a habit, seems like an arduous task. Maybe you have the best intentions to do it, but aren't set up for it. The result being, you just end up carrying on with the usual habit of wondering what to make for dinner, dashing out for something you just ran out of and spending too much time foraging in your cupboards.

A meal-planning system can be as basic or as systemized as your family needs. And make the grocery list based on that, to save time and money.

26. Use scraps of time efficiently.

We all experience scraps of time in our days that leave us with unavoidable delays and waits. Use these scraps of time for work or contemplation on your day's plans.

Always pack a book for snippets of reading pleasure and a pad of paper for note-taking. Making efficient use of scraps of time helps you to feel you're in control of how you use your time, instead of feeling at the mercy of waiting rooms or lines.

"In order to simplify my life and take better advantage of it, one of my most important efforts is time management. I schedule everything in order to get things done in a smooth way. I set aside a specific amount of time for specific things that are to be done every day. This way I don't need to rush through things."

—survey respondent

"The best way my wife and I have found to simplify our lives is to slow down. We make a very strong effort to NOT make plans at least 2 weekends per month, especially during the summer, so that we can enjoy our home and yard. Our friends are always complaining that they don't have a weekend free for the next 6 weeks, but we always have either next weekend or the following one free because of our planning."

—survey respondent

"To assist with wardrobe and time management, develop a roster for wearing your clothes. This can be applied for work, church and school. This has worked for me and helps me to maximize time."

—survey respondent

"Zen is not some kind of excitement, but concentration on our usual everyday routine."

—Shunryu Suzuki

"The secret of your future is hidden in your daily routine."

Books

Getting Things Done: The Art of Stress-Free Productivity by David Allen

Time Management from the Inside Out, second edition: *The Foolproof System for Taking Control of Your Schedule—and Your Life* by Julie Morgenstern

Services

This company handles written requests for removing a consumer's name and telephone number from most national telemarketing lists:

Telephone Preference Service
Direct Marketing Association
PO Box 9014
Farmingdale, NY 11735-9014

(Include your name, address and telephone number. Ask that your name is placed in the "delete" file.)

To register for the National Do Not Call Registry:
www.donotcall.gov/default.aspx

To reduce the amount of junk mail you receive, write to:

Mail Preference Service
Direct Marketing Association
PO Box 9008
Farmingdale, NY 11735-9008

To stop pre-approved credit card offers, call:

Trans Union
1-888-567-5688 (1-888-5-OPT-OUT)

Michael E. Angier

Chapter 3:
Enough Money—
Your Work and Your Income

It seems like a world without money would be the simplest of all. On the other hand, "enough" money for everyone would simplify things, too. One way or another, your money and how you earn and manage it are fundamental elements of your life and therefore an integral ingredient to your simplified life.

An old adage says that "money makes the world go 'round." Actually, gravity makes the world go 'round, but money can make your head spin when you don't have a handle on it. The following strategies will help to simplify your financial life so that your world doesn't need to revolve around it.

27. Live within your means.

This simplicity principle appears so obvious and yet far too many people don't live by it. Many people don't even know what their monthly budget looks like. Do you? Knowing the details of your budget and living within it can literally transform your life.

This principle is a major foundation point from which to build the kind of life you dream about. It all starts with a pencil, some paper and a calculator. Write down—in detail—your monthly expenses. Include dinners out, movie dates and daily cappuccinos. Include seasonal expenses like holiday spending or property taxes. Get real. See what's what, even if it scares you.

The secret is that it's far more frightening living outside of your means and not having a good, solid grasp on your budget. Once you get this in hand, you'll feel a strong sense of relief and empowerment.

28. Cut back on debt.

When was the last time you went into your bank and took a look at your various accounts? You may be surprised by the amount of service charges you pay each month.

Drop old, outdated accounts. Ask the teller to show you the features of different accounts and to help you select an account where you'll be paying the least for the set of features that suit you best.

Then there are those credit cards. Put your credit cards away in a place where you won't be able to use them until you're debt-free.

29. Consolidate debt.

Itemize all your debt: credit cards, consumer loans, etc. Then talk to your banker or credit union rep about consolidating these different debts into one and pay it off.

Don't close your credit card and loan accounts (your credit rating is higher if you show a record of open accounts with zero balances).

30. Pay off that debt.

One of the keys to financial solvency (and simplicity) is that no matter how much you make or how much you save, as long as you have debt—especially consumer debt—you aren't free. If you manage to pay off your debt, then there is no longer the pressure to achieve, and you can concentrate on what you really want out of life.

Here are some alarming stats: In the UK and the US, the average credit card debt exceeds $6,000. In the UK, the average debt (including mortgages) is equal to $18,000. 40% of American families spend more than they earn each month. There are more credit cards than there are people in Britain and America—with an average total of 4 credit cards per adult.

There are many various resources you can tap into for help and guidance on this topic. We've listed several at the end of this chapter.

31. Pay all your bills (on time).

If you're struggling to pay all your bills each month, you have two options: 1) reduce the number of bills you have or 2) increase your income enough to cover them. Do you really need all those magazine subscriptions or that book-of-the-month club membership? Are you really using all the services that you're paying for? Drop them if you don't use them.

A generation or two ago, most households had relatively simple bill-paying tasks. Nowadays, every family or household must implement some sort of system to manage bills—some sort of organized and regular system. As your bills enter your home, open them up, look at them and file them in whatever billing system you've set up. Around the same time each month, sit down with your bills file, a calculator and your checkbook (or computer, if you pay online). Pay them all or at least make the minimum payment. Then file the statements you may need for your records and throw out, recycle or shred the rest.

Don't let your bills go to collection! In fact, do whatever you need to do to prevent that from happening. The best and simplest strategy is to just call the company if you get a little behind. You may be surprised at how much help you can get from the company. After all, they want to keep you as a customer.

The amount of concern, worry and mental energy you'll free up when you're managing your bills well is the best pay off. And your life will be so much simpler.

32. Sign up for automatic bill paying.

Check with your bank or credit union to find out how to set up automatic deductions from your checking and/or savings account. Many banks and credit unions will even reduce the interest rate on loans you have with them if you request an automatic withdrawal from your in-house checking or savings account.

Ask your utility company, phone company, insurance company, mortgage company, etc., about their procedure to automatically deduct from your checking account the monthly bill amount. You'll not only simplify your regular bill-paying process, you'll save on the postage, too!

33. Reduce your nut.

We liked the way this strategy was worded. Your "nut" is the part of your monthly income required to support your lifestyle. A high-flying lifestyle would require a bigger nut than a simple one.

The thing about simplifying your finances is that your nut tends to grow and grow and grow over time as you continually add more expenses. This process can be quite gradual, so that you don't really take notice of how large and burdensome your income requirements have become.

Take stock of your monthly expense. Reduce it as much as possible, even a little bit at a time if you're unable or unwilling to make a drastic reduction. Shaving off nickels and dimes can be incredibly effective. Once you've got your nut down to a size that fits well with your income, you can remain conscious about not letting it grow.

34. Reduce monthly payments.

Furniture, electronics, cars, tools, appliances—so many things are all too easy to get these days, with no money down, pay-no-interest-till-next-century, bad-credit-is-okay offers. The stores make it so easy for you to come in and get more stuff (clutter), that you won't even notice how you're signing yourself and your family up for years and years of debt. You will most likely be paying for that furniture long after it's fallen apart.

If you can't afford it, don't get it. Or, save for it until you can buy it. Monthly payments for stuff (clutter) will just complicate your life with more bills, more debt, more worry, as well as more stuff to clean, maintain and store.

Let it go and see how simplicity can make you feel even better than you would have felt buying all that stuff.

35. Buy things for their usefulness.

One obvious marker of a simplified life is owning things for their function. Our culture encourages consuming just for the sake of consuming. The void is never filled by shopping, as promised.

So, one powerful strategy to simplify your life is to not buy things on the basis of that "feeling" you get from shopping. It's an empty feeling. Buy things you need, instead of things you want (or desire).

Mennonite, Quaker and Amish communities, for example, live simply and enjoy items in their homes that are simply functional. These objects (furniture and the like) are also very beautiful and have become highly prized in the market.

Look at your reasons for buying. You can gain more lasting fulfillment through other, deeper means.

36. Discover the Law of Attraction.

Abundance and prosperity are created from the inside out. The instant we are being abundant, prosperity will flow to us. The Law of Attraction, as defined by Abraham Hicks, states that "you attract to yourself what you give your attention and energy to, whether wanted or unwanted." We get what we focus on, so we might as well focus on our success.

Those people who seem to have all the "luck" and are blessed with abundance have simply become very efficient at attracting good things. They have learned it so well they may not even realize how exactly they do it.

We create our own reality. We attract those things in our life (money, relationships, employment) that we focus on. Life becomes much simpler when you understand this principle and when you begin to embrace it and use it.

37. Treat your money with respect.

If you want to increase your financial success, the best thing to start with is your cash. Take a look at how you carry, store and treat your actual physical cash. Do you have a wallet? Is it full of old, irrelevant bits? Do you crumple up your bills and stuff them into pockets? Are there piles of change lying around?

As financial guru Suze Orman says, "Respect your money and your money will respect you." This may seem like a trivial detail, but in truth, it's a powerful strategy. It fosters your potent and reciprocal relationship with money and, therefore, with your finances and, ultimately, with prosperity.

Try this: treat all bills and coins, even pennies, with equal respect. Keep cash tidy and organized in your wallet. Have a special place for loose change in your home. Don't disrespect cash by leaving it lying around your car, home and pockets. If you see a penny on the ground, pick it up and show it as much respect as you would a hundred-dollar bill. The point isn't that that coin will make a major difference in the amount of money you have, but that small action will strengthen your relationship with money. And an excellent relationship with money will increase the quality and simplicity of your life.

"We need to realize that life doesn't just revolve around financial means. Yes, it's necessary to have money. However, the most precious gifts in life are those that don't cost anything: love, care, appreciation. Success includes good health, energy and enthusiasm for life, relationships, creative freedom, well-being and peace of mind."

—survey respondent

"I am more deliberate about how I spend money. I carefully consider whether a purchase is a need or a want. If it is a want, it doesn't mean I won't purchase it, only that I consider the trade-offs and just what the "want" will satisfy and for how long, before it just becomes clutter."
—survey respondent

"Not what we have but what we enjoy constitutes our abundance."
—Epicurus

"When you are grateful, fear disappears and abundance appears."
—Anthony Robbins

Resources

9 Steps to Financial Freedom: Practical and Spiritual Steps So You Can Stop Worrying by Suze Orman

Law of Attraction by Michael Losier

The Attractor Factor : 5 Easy Steps for Creating Wealth (or Anything Else) from the Inside Out by Joe Vitale

Ask and It Is Given by Esther Hicks, Jerry Hick, and Wayne W. Dyer

Chapter 4:
What To Do—Add, Increase,
Practice, Learn, Do

At first, it may seem a bit counterintuitive to *add* things to do in order to make things simpler. However, the key is to add behaviors and habits that ultimately *reduce* the complexity of your life, instead of just increasing the length of your to-do list.

Voluntary simplicity, of course, is more than a series of new strategies to try. It's a new way of being in the world. Once you've decided to simplify things, you'll add a new layer of innovative thoughts and behaviors to your day. Soon, with repetition and practice, these will become habits. And these habits will form the foundation of your new nature.

38. Use a "not-to-do" list.

This strategy deserves emphasis. How many of us have ever-evolving "to-do" lists? How few of us actually make it all the way through our lists?

It seems there's no end of the tasks, duties and errands we *must* do in order to keep even a nominal grip on our busy and complex lives. And it's not very likely that your "to-do" list includes things such as:

✓ Smile more today
✓ Giggle helplessly at a child's antics
✓ Remember to breathe
✓ Give love
✓ Accept kindness

No, "to-do" lists are full of mundane drudgery that supposedly keeps our world from unraveling. They are a symptom of a too-busy, overly-complex and un-simple life.

Try the "*not* to-do" list! You'll love checking off each item at the end of the day.

39. Confront problems.

There are only two kinds of problems: those that will resolve eventually with little or no input and those that won't. Identify which problems require your attention (the ones that won't go away on their own). Then, simply attend to them. Avoiding them doesn't usually work. In fact, avoidance can complicate your life even further.

Take care of what needs taking care of. Attend to what needs attending to. It makes things much simpler to just take care of business. If you're not sure exactly what to do, ask for help, support or advice.

Most of the time, problems have a tendency of looming rather largely until we really face them down. Often, in the clear light of reason, problems shrink and become much more manageable.

40. Enjoy creation.

A foundation of a simple life is daily immersion in the natural world. Can you remember a night in your life (hopefully not in the too-distant past) when you sat back and pondered the night sky? Remember how that simplified things? The power of nature is awe-inspiring and there's nothing like a regular dose of awe to remind us how beautifully simple life truly is.

Whether you live near mountains, forest, desert or sea, take time to enjoy nature. Being outside, away from the appliances, machines and responsibilities of your indoor life is a treasure you can access any time. It will offer you balance, perspective and peace. It won't cost you a thing, you won't need any special equipment, you can share it with a loved one and it adds to every segment of your life in a positive way. The natural world is just outside your door, waiting for you to come outside and play.

41. Learn to say no in an assertive manner.

In order to live a truly simplified life and to maintain a satisfying level of simplicity with ease and grace, you need very clear boundaries. You need to set clear boundaries and be assertive about maintaining them. That means being assertive when it comes to saying "no." Many people have difficulty with this.

If you're one of those people, you don't like to "let others down," and you have a hard time saying no to almost any request that comes your way. Worse, you may jump in and offer a piece of yourself even before you're asked to.

Being assertive about your personal boundaries—about what you will and won't take on—means allowing yourself to say a big "yes" to your own chosen lifestyle.

Naturally, if you're able to help while maintaining your health, peace of mind and balance then, by all means do so. Voluntary simplicity does not preclude engaging with others and helping out when needed. But it does mean having a good sense of where your boundaries are and affirming them.

42. Take mini-vacations.

If you had 48 hours allotted to you for a vacation, what would you do? What would you do with 5 hours? If a vacation means getting away from the daily grind, relaxing a bit and laughing a lot, how can you do that without getting on a plane and maxing out your credit card?

The point of this strategy is to fit "vacations" into your regular routines. This works perfectly if you consider that a vacation can be a state of mind rather than a destination. What if your next day off was a holiday just for you? Use an afternoon or evening to be in vacation-mode.

Get away if you can, if it works well within a framework of voluntary simplicity. But why wait until that elusive two-week trip to the tropics appears? Your vacation is a state of mind.

As the person who submitted this strategy to our survey said: "Attempt to have more fun. Find a place where you can spend time thinking. Laugh at yourself."

43. Only participate and say "yes" to meaningful things.

When you have clear boundaries that are set by your personal values, you can be choosier about what events you put on your schedule. Being very clear about what fulfills you allows you to politely decline the next time you're asked to participate in something.

Drop events that don't mean much to you. Selectively participate in things that resonate with your values, background and goals. Getting involved in activities that are meaningful for you frees you from the self-doubt and worry that takes up so much of your time when your life is devoid of meaning.

Ask yourself four questions before accepting any obligation: Will this help me to reach my vision? Will this help me to accomplish any of my goals? Will I enjoy myself? Will this interfere with other obligations? Determine if this activity will fit your life based on your answers before committing yourself.

Searching for and finding meaning in your life simplifies your schedule, your responsibilities, your social life and your decision-making.

44. Say what you mean and do what you say.

This is another one of those "obvious" strategies, the kind of thing we teach to children. However, even though it's common sense, it can be a challenge to maintain. In the interest of correctness, politeness and an excess of "niceness", we often fall into a trap of saying what we think others want to hear, rather than saying what's in our hearts.

Many individuals suffer from a syndrome known colloquially as the "need to please disease." In their quest for approval and validation, they override their own measures of integrity in order to please anybody and everybody else. Not a very simple plan for life.

Living by a principle of saying what you mean and doing what you say removes much complication from your life. And amazingly, you'll still have friends; people will respect you for being true to yourself. Clearly, first you need to know what you mean in order to say it. This requires a level of self-awareness, which in itself is a bonus. Once you know what you mean, say it, do it and live by it.

45. Pause.

Before deciding a course of action, launching into a task or even making a comment, take a moment to center yourself. The velocity of our lives makes it difficult to pause, but as a learned skill, it will slow things down enough for you to make a difference in your life. It's as simple as taking a deep breathe or counting to 10. This gives you both the time and the centeredness to be in control and then to say what needs to be said or do what needs to be done.

We all know that it's wise to look before we leap and to think before we speak, but we rarely do either. A moment or two of pause provides you with power. That power will help you navigate your day in a new way with increased certainty, calm and wisdom.

46. Prepare a basic first-aid kit.

Emergency situations might not only complicate your life, but also end it—or that of a loved one. You can reduce the risk of injury and feel more prepared in a major emergency situation by learning some simple first-aid basics.

Prepare a basic first-aid kit and get first-aid training. You can purchase a pre-assembled first-aid kit in a store or put one together yourself.

Also, prepare a basic home emergency kit for a possible power outage, natural disaster or other emergency. Make sure to stock your home with an adequate supply of water, food, medications and other supplies.

And take your family through a trial fire alarm exercise. Your life is simplified with feeling prepared for the unex-pected.

47. Contribute.

When you are focused on "getting"—what you will get from a job, a business venture, a friendship, a romance, a family—you are putting yourself in an impoverished place where success does not thrive. This is a place of scarcity where there isn't enough love/money/opportunity/fortune to go around.

A fabulous strategy for shifting out of scarcity and into prosperity is to contribute. Focus instead on what you can give. Donate $20 to the food bank, volunteer an hour a month for a worthy cause, and give something of yourself. This reflects an attitude of abundance.

There is more than enough to go around. You have more than enough and can afford to give away. Almost instantly, success will find you.

"When I began starting the day saying "Namasté" and then silently saying "Namasté" whenever I encounter anyone, my life became much more pleasant and a lot simpler. It's easy and simple and once it becomes a habit, life flows. What better blessing can there be than honoring and blessing the Divinity within all of us? I find that Divinity honors me back when I do this habitually . . . my husband found that when he started doing this, people were less stressed and less negative and more cooperative, positive and fun! Life just keeps getting better and better and simpler, too!"

—survey respondent

"Life is complex at best. The purpose in everyone's life is to live it to its fullest. To help accomplish this goal and to simplify life, take time out to enjoy it. Take walks in nature. Listen to the birds sing. Watch the sunrise. Enjoy the moment. Turn off the TV and read a book. You'll save electricity and you might just learn a thing or two."

—survey respondent

Michael E. Angier

"I think one of the best ways to simplify life is to just sit quietly at the end of the day and listen to the quiet. This, of course, means finding a very quiet spot, but that action in itself is therapeutic."

—survey respondent

"Breathe. Let go. And remind yourself that this very moment is the only one you know you have for sure."

—Oprah Winfrey

Websites

Federal Emergency Management Agency (FEMA)
www.fema.gov/

Books

The Assertiveness Workbook: How to Express Your Ideas and Stand Up for Yourself at Work and in Relationships by Randy J. Paterson Ph.D.

Coward's Guide to Conflict: Empowering Solutions for Those Who Would Rather Run Than Fight by Tim Ursiny

Chapter 5:
What Not To Do—
Avoid, Reduce, Stop, Let Go, Move On

If your hands are so full that your days are a juggling act, it's time to drop something. You just can't continue picking things up and adding them to your tasks. You need to know when and what to let go, so that your life transforms into a simpler one.

This chapter describes ideas for decreasing complexities in your life. It requires the ability and the willingness to stop, drop, and yes, even avoid certain things. These strategies will help you develop your "not to-do list."

48. Don't react.

A law of physics states that for every action there is an equal and opposite reaction. Fortunately, human interactions don't abide by laws of physics.

One of the keys to reducing stress and increasing the quality of relationships is to stop reacting. This is one of those things that is much easier than it sounds, but the results are definitely worth it. Instead of reacting, simply respond.

Learn to replace your knee-jerk reaction with a response. In every interaction there is that moment, an instant just before you're about to react. That moment holds a lot of power for you. That's the instant for you to choose your response. It's the time for you to pause, take a breath or two and consider your options. Only then do you respond, with genuineness, integrity and consideration.

When you choose to respond, rather than react, you're moving forward with clarity and deliberation, instead of pushing back in irritation, doubt or thoughtlessness. Your relationships, communication and your interpersonal results will be better for it.

49. Let it go.

When faced with all those complications and situations of daily life, it's good to remember that we always have the option of simply letting go. We all experience daily frustrations with family, jobs and the little complications that challenge us on a daily basis.

The biggest mistake we make in dealing with these frustrations is dwelling on them and blowing them out of proportion. It's much easier to just let go and move forward towards our goals. Of course, you can't always let go of the circumstances (or the people!) in your life, but you can always choose to let go of the frustrations and worry around them.

You don't need to carry it all along with you as you try to achieve your goals. It's OK for you to decide to put some things down, in order to be able to have a better hold on what's important to you. Give yourself permission to let some things go.

50. Turn it down.

There is a lot of noise in today's world. At home, in the car, in malls, cafés and restaurants, there seems to be blaring music, ads and voices everywhere. On top of that, there are the ambient noises of traffic and construction.

One way to gain balance, peace and a measure of simplicity is to turn down the noise as much as possible. On your drive to work, you can keep the radio off and enjoy that time in silence. Or at home, if the TV or radio is on but no one is attending to them, turn them off.

In some homes, background noise seems to be preferred, with the TV on all day. That can just fill your mind with buzz and clatter that robs you of your sense of calm. When you're not calm, you can hardly experience simplicity.

51. Turn it off.

One of the most common responses to our simplicity survey was the suggestion to eliminate television from your life as much as possible. Yes, it can be informative and entertaining. But let's be honest, the vast majority of the time it's nothing more than a mindless distraction and time-waster. Even with hundreds of channels to choose from, there is usually not much to watch that genuinely adds to the quality of your life. And it certainly detracts from family-life and other inter-personal relationships. It's far better to interact with your friends and family than spending time sitting in front of another sitcom.

So, turn it off for a night or a week or even a month. There is so much more for yourself, for your family and even for the world.

52. Try a "News Diet."

Even the daily habit of watching the evening news (or reading the newspaper) can detract from a simple life. There is just so much information that our minds can process before we begin to feel the symptoms of the dreaded information overload. However, we can choose to filter the information we're taking in.

One effective way is to reduce our news intake—either on an ongoing basis or for a temporary period. An added benefit to a news diet is that it drastically reduces the amount of bad news we're absorbing. Yes, it's important to be informed and to remain relevant, but it's not necessary to allow ourselves to be inundated with terrible stories each and every evening.

This strategy is not about tuning out completely or about staying out of touch, but about putting a healthy limit on the bad news sifting through our minds each day.

53. Don't worry.

"Don't worry; be happy" makes a nice jingle, but what about a life strategy? Usually it falls under the category of "Easier Said Than Done." However, it *is* a basic truth that worry acts like prayer in reverse. The more you focus on the outcome that you're worrying about, the more you attract that outcome toward your life. Worrying, fretting, stewing, agonizing—these all-too-common activities—rarely help anything.

Worry is an added burden that steals the very reserves you need to solve the problem in the first place. There is something to be said for just *enough* worry: just enough worry can impel you to take action and make change. Just enough worry can give you the energy to solve a problem. But burdening yourself (and those around you) with ongoing worry is debilitating. Give it up.

54. Park it.

Several of our survey respondents submitted strategies regarding driving less. We live in a car culture, and most of us rely heavily on driving in our day-to-day routines. However, leaving the car idle in the garage can be a strategy for simplicity.

Think about all the logistics it takes to run your car: maintenance, gas, navigating traffic, road rage. You can leave all that behind for a day or so. While it's true that your car will simplify your life in some ways, it can also complicate it. So give it a rest once in a while.

One survey respondent suggested: "Once in a while, park the car on Friday and don't start it up until Monday." A weekend without driving may be just what you need to add a small measure of simplicity to your life.

55. Ignore them.

Paying less attention to what other people do, say and expect was a popular suggestion from our survey. Several respondents said that our consumer society's guiding principle of "keeping up with the Joneses" was the cause of too much stress, complications and overwhelm. Others said that too much attention on the actions and words of others takes the focus away from our own goals and values.

Those responses suggested allowing for a reasonable consideration of outside influences (advice, comments, criticisms, etc.), but ultimately adhering to our own set of principles and decisions. Spending your life trying to live up to another person's expectations for you will inevitably lead to stress, overwhelm and a loss of your own life's direction. Once you get clear on your own direction, your own values, passions and goals, you have a path to follow that is your own.

56. Go with the flow.

If life was a river, there are some people who cling fearfully to the banks and never get anywhere; there are some who use up all their strength swimming against the stream; yet others who paddle along in the flow of the current. Which kind of life-swimmer are you? We all know individuals who easily go with the flow. Maybe you are one of those fortunate people. People who can flow with the currents of life really do experience more ease and simplicity. They don't struggle as much and don't get caught up in the shallows while life flows on by.

Going with the flow is a dramatic strategy to implement. It is vital to maintain a strong sense of self and good boundaries and a sense of assertiveness, but to generally move easily through and past things. Go with the flow and see where the current takes you—it's simpler that way.

57. Stop blaming others now.

Guess what? Life isn't happening to you. Instead, you're creating your own life. You are not a passive victim of life, of society or of other people. *You* are in charge of your experience, no one else. Never give that power away.

A sure sign that you're playing the victim's role is that you blame others for the circumstances in your life or blame others for how you feel about those circumstances. Even if you have been a victim, or if you are currently a victim, you can stop right now. Become a survivor. The instant you stop blaming others, you take back your power. Your life becomes simpler.

"I think my attachments are making my life more complicated. Detaching myself from things, not looking at the result and enjoying the process is the secret."

—survey respondent

"Let go. Let go of the past. Let go of the future. Live today. Let go of the hurt. Let go of the pain. Let go."

—survey respondent

"Everything in the universe has a cycle to it. From geological cycles spanning millions of years, to the mating cycle of a gnat—everything cycles, even you. Become more aware of your own natural cycles and quit fighting against the flow. I've learned that for several weeks I am a whirlwind of ideas and productivity, followed by a brief period of rest and inner reflection. I've learned to recognize these cycles and feel a lot less angst. Even financial prosperity has a flow. Learn to recognize your financial cycles and you won't sweat so much when money is at ebb tide. Flow tide always follows!"

—survey respondent

"I believe that you control your destiny, that you can be what you want to be. You can also stop and say 'No, I won't do it; I won't behave this way anymore.'"

—Leo Buscaglia

Books

Sleep Thinking: The Revolutionary Program That Helps You Solve Problems, Reduce Stress, and Increase Creativity While You Sleep by Eric, Maisel, Ph.D., Natalya Maisel

How to Stop Worrying and Start Living, by Dale Carnegie

Michael E. Angier

Chapter 6:
Make the Connections—Your
Relationships

The songs say that love makes the world go round, all you need is love and what the world needs now is love, love.

Unless you're living as a hermit on a remote mountainside (in which case your life is already quite simple!), your day is filled with human interactions. If you choose the path of a simpler life, you'll eventually need to address those connections. Relationships—the good, the bad and the weird—make up so much of our lives that they simply cannot be ignored. Here are some strategies offered by our survey participants that can help you simplify the relationships in your life.

58. Surround yourself with positive people.

Sometimes it isn't so much the circumstances that add frustration, uncertainty and negativity to your life, but the people. A good reflection of where you're at in life is the group of people you associate with most.

Take a clear look at the individuals you surround yourself with. Do they tend to uplift you, support you and add positive energy to your life? Or do they drag you down with complaints and negative attitudes?

Take a good look at the people surrounding the successful and happy people you know. In all probability, they surround themselves with dynamic, positive individuals. This isn't just by coincidence.

True, you can't choose your family, but you can choose who impacts your life and who enters your personal space. Gravitate toward people who behave the way you wish to be and who do the things you dream of doing.

Seek out those with attitudes that will enhance your life, not detract from it. Cut negative people out of your life as much as possible. The politics of dealing with such people can be very complicated and exhausting, often requiring more effort than it's worth. Surround yourself with positive, dynamic people. You'll soon find your own attitude and your own life transform in positive ways.

59. Don't gossip

Nobody likes gossip; yet almost everybody does it. Everybody understands how negative it is; yet hardly anybody boycotts it. Unfortunately, gossip seems to fulfill a basic human need for validation and esteem. We unconsciously use gossip to inflate ourselves with negative talk about others.

Gossip taints the workplace, the family and the community. Every time you participate in gossip, either by dishing or by listening, you perpetuate the negativity. Each time you have the courage to walk away or otherwise halt gossip, you're nurturing positive relationships and circumstances. It's as simple as that.

The practice of non-participation in gossip can be difficult at first. And it gets easier with practice. Eventually, it's one of the habits of your simplified life.

60. Let relationships go.

Just because you were friends once doesn't mean you're pledged to be friends all your life. Yes, long-lasting and even lifelong friendships are to be cherished. But only a very few friendships will make that grade.

In many cases, friends come along during particular periods in our lives and then naturally fade away when we (or they) evolve to new levels. And that is not only appropriate but perfectly natural.

Relationships are meant to nurture your spirit, to support your growth. Once they no longer mutually fulfill that role, it's okay to allow them to dissolve. Sometimes, it's best for simplicity's sake to let go of relationships.

61. Take responsibility.

A survey respondent put it very succinctly: "Life would be simpler for everyone if everyone took responsibility for their own lives, instead of looking for someone else to blame." Taking responsibility for one's own words and actions is a founding standard of maturity and honor.

We need to own our decisions and be accountable for the consequences of our words and actions. We all make mistakes. It takes an individual who is confident in their values and certain of their integrity to stand up and acknowledge an error and to make the changes necessary to fix the situation. It takes a steadfast and honorable person to look at how their decisions have affected others and to claim responsibility for the outcome, either good or bad.

Too much energy is spent in complaining about others and in wailing about situations, when it could be better spent in acknowledging our part in the results. It's true. If we all stood up and took responsibility for our own lives, actions and decisions, the world would be much simpler.

62. Change.

Mahatma Gandhi may have said it best: "Be the change you want to see in the world." Take a look at your life. If you want to see more motivation, motivate others. If you want to see more kindness, be kind to someone. If you want more love, give more love. It's an exceedingly simple plan and yet it seems so elusive to many of us.

In order to change the world, change yourself first. The purpose of life is for you to grow and develop as a human being. You're here to further yourself, not in the way of property or status, but in the way of personal evolution. Along the way, you'll be forced to make changes.

Life can't happen without some transformations along the way. Rather than grumbling about how others should change or how situations need changing, work on yourself. By making change in yourself, either momentous or subtle, you'll be the spark for greater change in the world. In fact, the simple secret is that once you make the changes you want so much to see in the world, the world will follow.

63. Be neighborly.

Living a simple life doesn't mean becoming remote and isolated from the world. A rich and simple life includes community, partnerships, friends and family. It also includes great neighbors. How do you get great neighbors? Be one. Get to know your neighbors. Offer to help when they're working on a project and don't hesitate to request help when you need a hand. Positive neighbor relationships foster the kind of community that adds simplicity to our lifestyles in a variety of ways.

Consider what you can do to establish or build better relationships with your neighbors. Suggestions from our survey include: host a potluck get-together; call your neighbors every so often; visit or invite them for a visit; lend a helping hand; ask for a helping hand; hand out cards for holidays; spend an extra five minutes chatting when you see them in the street. Whatever way you find to foster neighbor relations, you'll be fostering a richer neighborhood.

64. Forgive.

Forgiveness is a profound subject, one that takes up much more discussion than we can include here. It's the source of grace, some say, and the result of sound personal evolution.

A measure of forgiveness will transform a life more than virtually anything else. It releases energy, clears anger, relieves anguish, heals the heart. To forgive others of their crimes against you is to set yourself free; even though it in no way suggests that the harm done to you was acceptable.

To forgive yourself is to clear a new road ahead of you. Forgive yourself for hurting others (either intentionally or not), for not taking action when action was called for, for ignoring an injustice, for being weak when strength was needed.

Forgiveness is the key to release you from the past and allow you to move forward, unfettered along your personal journey through life. Forgiveness releases your tie to the person and to the event. Forgiveness will free you. Forgive yourself while you're at it.

65. Family first.

You may have heard that blood is thicker than water. For many, our blood-ties have the most significance in our lives; our families are a source of life-giving benefit. Spend more time with your family. It's so simple, yet makes such a difference.

If you believe that you don't have the time, you need to re-examine your schedule. There is nothing more worthy than setting aside the time and space to be with those you love and who love you.

Survey respondents offered these suggestions for putting your family first: Limit the number of activities away from home; Have dinner together each night; Spend less time with things that don't matter; Focus outside duties while the kids are in school and then be with them when they are home.

Do whatever it takes and reap the benefits. At the end of your life, there will not be one minute you spent with your family that you'll regret.

66. Ask about it.

When in comes to relationships, one of the most significant keys for success is communication. Everyone is challenged by relationships; they're not always easy. Our relationships with our significant others can be especially fraught and demand the best of us. Obviously, the rewards of a solid partnership are many; it's always worth the work you put into it.

There is a strategy for simplifying the communication in a relationship. It involves just one simple question: What can I do to be more supportive? This one question has the power to cut through much frustration and misunderstanding. It gets right to the heart of the matter. It shows your partner that you have the willingness to do what it takes to make things better. It also helps you figure out the best direction to move forward in the relationship. "What can I do to be more supportive?" is a question that opens up doors of possibilities. You can vitalize all your relationships with it. What a simple way to enhance your life.

67. Ask for it.

Once in a while you need a helping hand. We're human and that means that we don't go through this life isolated from the rest of the race. There are as many sorts of lifestyles as there are individuals and each one, without exception, requires assistance sometimes. Whether it's help with a difficult task, advice on a tricky dilemma or support through tough times, we all need it, like it or not.

The problem is that it can be very hard to reach out and ask for the help you need. We carry around a fallacy that needing (and asking for) help is a display of weakness. Not so. Getting help when you need it is a sign of inner strength, not to mention intelligence.

Think about a time when your own assistance was required. Maybe someone asked you for help or maybe you saw a need and reached out to help on your own. Did you think any less of the person you helped? Of course not. Was it a negative experience that made you resentful? Of course not.

The act of helping others is a positive and enriching act. Therefore, on the other side of things, asking for and accepting help is also positive and enriching. So let go of false beliefs and ask for help when you need it. People will be honored that you asked and happy to assist in whatever way they can, just like you would be.

68. Be human.

Although we rely a great deal on technology and many of us strive for something near perfection, it's vital to remember that we're human. And as human, we're delightfully flawed, wonderfully quirked and far from perfect. The irony is that our innate "imperfections" are the elements that make us perfectly human.

Don't expect flawless results of yourself or of others. Allow for the missteps and the head-over-heels tumbles through life.

If you spend your life fighting against the imperfections in yourself and in those around you, what kind of life will you have? Simplify by accepting your humanity. The beauty of each unique individual lies in their differences. That goes for you, too. As a survey respondent said, "You are an imperfect, flawed, quirky, unique human being. So are the rest of us. Accept it (revel in it, even!) and you will be more at peace."

"When I watched less TV and chatted more with my kids, my life got a lot simpler!"
—survey respondent

"Say what you mean and mean what you say."
—survey respondent

"Treasure your relationships, not your possessions."
—Anthony J. D'Angelo, *The College Blue Book*

"Without relationships, no matter how much wealth, fame, power, prestige and seeming success by the standards and opinions of the world one has, happiness will constantly elude him."

—Sidney Madwed

Books

Relationship Rescue by Phillip C. McGraw

The 7 Habits of Highly Effective Families by Sandra Merrill Covey

Michael E. Angier

Chapter 7:
Alter Your Focus—Your Attitude

Your mental attitude is truly the source of so much of your experience of the world. How you are in the world dictates the world you live in. Cynics live in a cynical world; the frightened live in a hostile world; the doubtful live in an uncertain world.

Fortunately, while we have very little influence over the world itself, we have absolute influence over our own attitudes. Remember, the merry live in a cheerful world; the compassionate live in a loving world; the adventuresome live in a thrilling world.

What kind of world do you live in?

69. Get clear.

One of the principles of the SuccessNet creed is: "Clarity is power." The clearer we are about our strengths and weaknesses, our limitations and possibilities and our goals, the better our lives will be.

To become vividly clear on your passions and values is to discover the easiest road to the fulfillment of your dreams. To know your goals with detailed clarity is half the journey to achieve them.

Clear communication enhances relationships. Developing a clear picture of your dreams-come-true will expedite your realization of them. When you're not clear, your energy will be weaker and scattered.

Your goals will be elusive. It's worth taking the time to sit and get a clear focus on things: your values, passions and priorities; on your goals and potential; on your life. Clarity leads to power—and to a simpler way of life.

70. Accept what is.

Sometimes, just saying "Yes" to whatever you're facing will clear the way before you. We tend to spend much time and energy resisting and denying the way things are, when simple acceptance would free us from a lot of struggle.

Once we can truly accept things for what and how they are, we free up energy to deal with them. As author and talk show host Dr. Phil says, "You can't change what you don't acknowledge."

On a deeper level, when you can accept even the most difficult circumstances, you will gain just enough distance from them to be able to get a clearer perspective and to make better decisions about moving beyond them.

Giving a resounding "Yes!" to challenges (and to challenging people) is a powerful strategy for empowering and simplifying your life. It's not easy, but it is simple: Accept it.

71. Breathe.

Seriously. Breathe. Take a deep breath right now. Take a few more. Repeat as necessary. Breathing fully will make you feel more calm, content and confident. Breathing deeply gives you perspective, clarity and focus. It centers your thoughts, energizes your body and calms your nerves.

Several times a day, take the 60 seconds or so that you need to breathe fully a few times. The trick is to become aware of your breathing and to implement a trigger to remind yourself to take a few deep breaths. For example, breathe fully each time you stop at a red light or every time you wash your hands. Not only will it not hurt, it will feel great. It's giving yourself a moment of serenity in the midst of chaos. It's a gift to yourself of health, ease and clear thinking.

Breathing is more than a mechanism for keeping your body alive. Deep, conscious breathing is a powerful means to achieve your ultimate state of being.

72. Be happy.

A survey respondent wrote, "One of the ways by which I have personally been able to achieve simplicity, to a large extent, is by making a conscious effort to be happy no matter what the circumstances surrounding me are." The brilliance in this approach to simplicity is that it removes the need to "pursue" happiness. It implies that happiness is forever within our reach, always accessible.

You needn't wait for circumstances to align themselves just right in order to be happy. You have the option of being happy right *now*, in the precise set of circumstances you currently face. Happiness, in fact, may not prove to be elusive after all; we can experience it the moment we choose to.

And smile. Smiling can simplify relationships on a fundamental level. As one survey respondent put it, "When you're feeling secure and happy, let your face know about it."

Furthermore, just because you're striving to better your life doesn't mean that contentment is impossible. You can be content in your present state while you work toward transforming your life. You don't have to wait until you achieve this goal or that lifestyle in order to know happiness. It's yours now.

73. Know the difference.

One key to experiencing simplicity is to learn to recognize the difference between the important and the insignificant. Once we can separate the two in our lives, we can focus and resolve the significant and drop whatever is of no consequence to us. This strategy simplifies our daily routines and our responsibilities, as well as our mental and emotional experiences.

The principle behind this strategy is reflected in a well-known saying known as the Serenity Prayer, used in many Alcoholics Anonymous groups: "God, grant me the serenity to accept the things I cannot change, courage to change the things I can, and wisdom to know the difference." This colloquial prayer is grounded in pastoral and psychological wisdom; countless of thousands have learned to live by these words and, in doing so, have achieved a new measure of simplicity in their lives.

Comments on this theme from our simplicity survey included: "Don't take inconsequential things too seriously"; "Resolve to leave fretting to others"; "When we become fretful, our wheels are just spinning. We waste enormous energy getting nowhere."

So, refuse to waste energy on the inconsequential. Save it for what is really important.

74. Get aligned.

To live most simply, day in and day out, you must align all your thoughts, words and deeds. What you say becomes aligned with what you're thinking—say what you mean. What you do is aligned with what you say—do what you say you'll do. Your decisions, actions and habits become harmonious with thought and word. To achieve this standard of alignment takes a good deal of self-awareness and commitment. However, like every skill, it becomes easier with practice.

When you're more aligned, you'll feel calmer and more confident in your decisions. A degree of serenity is one of the benefits. On the other hand, living out of alignment creates confusing emotions and chaotic situations. Save yourself the trouble and pay attention to how aligned your thoughts, words and deeds are on a daily basis.

75. Decide.

We've all experienced the agony of indecision. It can be paralyzing. Not knowing what decision to make can also be disheartening and frustrating. Most of the time, we experience these negative feelings because we're not sure how our decisions will turn out. It's the results of our decisions we fear, not the actual decisions.

There are always consequences to our decisions. And as adults, we make decisions all the time, some major, some minor. Learning to trust yourself with making a decision will simplify your life in many ways.

Fortunately, you don't need to know the ultimate outcome of your decision in order to make one. When you make a decision based on your best judgment of the facts at hand, your decision is a good one, no matter what the outcome. Make a choice and move on.

Decision-making is a key to simplicity. And remember, if the results of your decisions are not what you're hoping for, you'll be able to make a new set of decisions regarding what to do about it.

76. Practice optimism.

Pessimism kills dreams dead. You must shift to optimism if you want to live your best—and most simple—life. It's all in the mind, and it's possible to be realistic and practical while maintaining optimism.

Professor Martin Seligman, author of *"The Optimistic Child,"* describes an important distinction between how an optimist views events versus a pessimist: A pessimist views an event through a filter of "the 3 P's"; that is, the event is seen as personal, permanent and pervasive. An optimist, on the other hand, views events as impersonal, temporary and specific. An optimistic person believes in the innate goodness of people and the benign-ness of the universe. As one survey respondent suggested: "indulge in the magic of believing."

77. Choose your battles.

A survey respondent said that he simplified his life by "choosing my battles carefully, instead of fighting every one that comes my way." This is a very straightforward tactic for clearing out superfluous complications from your life.

Whenever you're faced with the possibility of a confrontation, struggle, altercation or battle, take the time to ask if this is one you wish to "fight." Will this interaction improve or enhance things? Will it increase or diminish the simplicity in your life? Often, it makes more sense to just walk away.

You'll lose energy, time and resources by engaging in each and every "battle" that comes your way. Be in control of which ones you engage in; your relationships will be more peaceful and your life simpler.

"Don't fret over the frivolous or get tense over the trivial."

—survey respondent

"I've trained myself to realize that I cannot possibly please everybody or meet every need, and so I do what falls in line with my life's mission and leave the rest alone."

—survey respondent

"I try to exchange every negative thought for a positive one and that alone makes everything simpler for me."

—survey respondent

"Develop an attitude of gratitude and give thanks for everything that happens to you, knowing that every step forward is a step toward achieving something bigger and better than your current situation."

—Brian Tracy

"Any fact facing us is not as important as our attitude toward it, for that determines our success or failure. The way you think about a fact may defeat you before you ever do anything about it."

—Norman Vincent Peale

Book

Attitude is Everything : 10 Life-Changing Steps to Turning Attitude Into Action, by Keith Harrell

Chapter 8:
Be Balanced—Your Health
and Well-Being

All of your possessions, relationships, hobbies and re-sponsibilities—each and every one of them—are en-tirely dependent on the maintenance of your own health. Your to-do lists and clutter-busting strategies suddenly mean little if you're faced with a health crisis. Pay attention to how balanced your life is; your health depends on it. And so much depends on your health, doesn't it?

78. Journal.

The act of writing down your impressions, musings and problems is a powerful strategy to get a handle on whatever circumstances you're in.

Getting it out of your head and onto paper helps you see more clearly into what may seem indecipherable or confus-ing. Besides that, the *action* of writing uses new neurological pathways that can help you gain a different perspective on what you're writing about.

Journaling just takes paper and pen; it's free, low-tech and simple. It provides you with a few minutes of peace and clarity. It's a form of meditation. It's good for your mental and emotional well-being.

The effects of journaling will aid your relationships and solve your problems. Your journal writing will be as unique as you are—no need to live up to any standards of literature

74

or grammar! Be yourself in your journal and you'll discover a lot more about just who that 'self' is.

79. Meditate.

No discourse on simplicity is complete without a mention of meditation. A regular program of meditation—just a few minutes at a time—makes an enormous difference to your life. Meditation brings peace to a hectic day, perspective to a confusing situation, clarity to an obscure problem.

Obviously, there are many methods of meditation, but the basic premise is to deliberately slow down, focus on your breathing and clear your mind of distractions. No need to struggle or strain at it; meditation is a gentle act.

And it takes practice. The first few times you try it, it will likely be quite difficult. Don't push yourself to "perform" at meditation. Simply allow yourself the space to practice. It will get easier. Let meditation become a habit and allow yourself to be open to the possibilities.

80. Ask for support.

With all the juggling that we do—work, family, financial and social responsibilities—it's so easy to get overwhelmed. Yet for some reason, many of us will go along, feeling over-whelmed, drowning in tasks and not say a word. Why? Maybe we've been conditioned to keep things to ourselves, especially the more "difficult" emotions. Perhaps we believe we'll appear weak if we let our frailties show. It could also be that we've been taught to go through difficulties alone.

For whatever reason, too many of us have extreme difficulty reaching out for (and accepting) a helping hand. Don't be scared to ask for help— you don't have to take on the whole burden by yourself. There is no weakness—not even the smallest degree—in asking for support.

It takes courage and intelligence to get help when you need it. Asking for support is a sign of a balanced and healthy mind. People tend to be helpful by nature. We *want* to help.

81. Have some fun.

There are certain individuals who lead their lives based on a credo of having fun, as though fun were the *point* of being alive. Focusing one's life solely on the pursuit of fun times isn't exactly a balanced way to go. However, having fun, experiencing joy, being amused and entertained are all important aspects of a full, rich (and simple) life.

When was the last time you had loads of fun? Stop and think about it. When was the last time you really enjoyed yourself? What were you doing? Who were you with?

Laughter, fun and pure enjoyment have the shared characteristic of clearing out the mental, emotional and physical cobwebs. It's healthy to have fun regularly; it's good for you. Add fun to your new, simpler life. Make it part of your new routine.

82. Take a walk.

Did you know that, physically speaking, the human body is engineered to walk? Walking, more than running, standing or sitting is the action for which our bodies are in perfect balance, alignment and purpose. You are designed for walking. Maybe that's why walking feels so good!

In our car culture, we don't walk so much anymore, but it's an activity to add to your life that is rich in benefits. Mentally, there's nothing like a stroll or a hike to gain perspective. Emotionally, it literally blasts depression or lethargy.

Physically, of course, there is almost nothing better for you. Financially, well, it's free. Socially, walking together can form strong bonds between people.

So let your body do what it's designed to do. Take a walk.

83. Get dirty.

Another practice of a simple life is gardening. Whether it's a vegetable patch, a flower bed or a container of herbs, gardening is an activity that connects you to a simpler way of life.

It's pretty hard to feel frenetic and overwhelmed after five minutes of deadheading marigolds or weeding between the radishes. Not only is it inherently soothing, but gardening is also very rewarding. After all, it's tapping into the life-force and nurturing life.

If you don't consider yourself a gardener, consider this: gardening is a multi-*billion* dollar industry in North America alone. There must be a good reason for all that commerce!

Luckily, dirt is cheap, and it's a hobby or pastime that has low financial impact. It's also an excellent way to connect socially, by sharing seeds and your harvest, be it all those extra zucchinis or a bouquet of wildflowers. Get your hands in the dirt to add yet another dimension of simplicity to your life.

84. Take care.

Self-care is an integral aspect of a good life. However, all too often it's shunted to the very end of a long list of responsibilities.

Furthermore, we may also struggle with feelings of guilt when we use the time and energy to take proper care of ourselves—as though self-care were a selfish indulgence. It isn't.

When you take care of your children's parent (you), you're enriching their lives. When you take care of your significant other's partner (you again), you're improving the quality of your relationship. When you take care of yourself, you're taking care of everything, from your work and your family to your community. Self-care is not an indulgence.

A decent night's sleep is a sound health principle, not excessive pampering. Likewise, proper nourishment and exercise are basic tenets of health.

How does self-care make your life simpler? When your health is attended to, with proper rest, food and exercise, you'll have more energy and ability to attend to other things in your life. A balanced, healthy life is a simpler life.

85. Be here now.

A universal truth is that the present moment is the only place from which we can make change. When you're stuck in the past, spending much of your energy ruminating over past regrets, you'll have very little energy left over to make any changes in the present.

The same goes for the future. If you focus mostly on future-time, on upcoming events or waiting for something to arrive, you'll be robbed of the power of the present moment.

The only moment you have is now. When you can begin to take literally the instruction "Be Here Now", your life will adjust itself. It takes clear intention and perseverance. It takes practice. But learning to live in the *now* is a powerful strategy to tap into. Whenever you can be grounded and centered in the present moment, most of your problems and perceived fears will recede.

86. Stay in integrity.

Things can get very complicated if you live your life out of integrity. Virtually nothing else will increase the chaos, disarray and disorder in a life than functioning outside of one's integrity.

According to the dictionary, integrity is the possession and steadfast adherence to one's moral principles and standards, as well as a state of being whole, complete. Integrity can be tricky to describe, but it is instantly recognizable. It's also easy to see when someone is out of integrity.

Learn to recognize what it feels like to be out of integrity. When you are out of alignment with your own unique sense of truth, values, ethical principles and moral character, you will feel "off." That's the clue that you need to re-align with your own moral standards.

Being steadfast and true to one's integrity is reward in itself; however, it also produces symptoms of increased satisfaction, peace and simplicity in one's life. As one survey respondent said of integrity: "Do what you need to do to remain in integrity and fortune will smile upon you."

87. Be honest.

Tell the truth. As Mark Twain said, "If you tell the truth, you don't have to remember anything." Honesty keeps your life simple. A lie can easily grow into a stack of lies to cover up your first lie. How complicated is that?

Make a decision to always tell the truth, even if your first instinct is to cover it with a lie. One survey respondent said she "made a recent decision to always speak the truth about anyone and anything. Now her friends think her golf game has deteriorated because she's no longer lying about her score."

If you find yourself telling someone a lie or embellishing an event, correct it as soon as possible, no matter how awkward you may feel. And avoid lying to make yourself or others feel better. Deep down, they know the truth and will respect you more for being a true friend—and being honest.

88. Express your creativity.
Get back to expressing your creativity. Remember the beautiful music you strummed with your guitar or the romantic poem you wrote your loved one that brought tears to her eyes?

You can reveal your creativity in many wonderful ways: through your music, needlepoint, the gourmet meal you make, the flowers you arrange. Simplicity, beauty, comfort and harmony flow in and through one another.

89. Charge up.
Ever felt burnt out from work, relationship and life? We all get that way sometimes. That burnt-out feeling—lack of enthusiasm, motivation, focus and energy—is a sign that we haven't been attending to self-care. It means it's time to recharge.

One way to look at yourself is that you're made up of reserves of energy, like batteries. You have a work battery, a family battery, a self battery, a health battery and so on. Every now and then, just like regular batteries, your energy in one particular reserve drops, likely due to overuse.

Too much time and resources expended on the work front, for example, will de-charge your work battery: if the charge drops critically low, you'll feel burnt out. The same happens to your health, family and other reserves.

The burnt-out feeling is actually a helpful hint that it's time to recharge your batteries. Be sure to build and maintain your reserves in all areas of your life. When your reserves become empty, all kinds of negative results can ensue, including health issues. Recharge your batteries and keep them topped up.

"Have the courage to be independent and out of touch sometimes. By this I mean, stop being a slave to the phone and emails. The constant interruptions mean that we are 'firefighting' all the time and not actually being effective and achieving our goals. One of the happiest people I know doesn't have a mobile phone or a computer—he's able to go about doing the things he needs to do, as well as the things he enjoys, without constantly being pulled at! Also, he has excellent friendships since he has quality time to spend with his friends. Put simply: just switch off!"

—survey respondent

"Don't let everything get to you, especially when you're stressed . . . laugh lots, keep a positive attitude and keep that smile on your face, don't stress over the small stuff, pick your battles."

—survey respondent

"In all things of nature there is something of the marvelous."
—Aristotle, Greek critic, philosopher, physicist, & zoologist

"So divinely is the world organized that every one of us, in our place and time, is in balance with everything else."
—Johann Wolfgang von Goethe, novelist, poet & scientist

Report

Raising the Bar: Increasing Your Standards of Excellence
eBooklet, in PDF format, free to readers

This report shows you how to make positive and lasting changes—changes that will enhance your life and work. This report teaches the why and the how of raising your standards and creating excellence.

www.SuccessNet.org/o-standards

Books

Feeling Good: The Science of Well-Being by C. Robert Cloninger

True Balance : A Commonsense Guide for Renewing Your Spirit by Sonia Choquette

How to Meditate: A Guide to Self-Discovery by Lawrence LeShan

The Secret to Being Fiercely Focused by Michael E. Angier

Michael E. Angier

Chapter 9: Know Thyself—
Your Self-Awareness

What could be simpler than knowing yourself? Well, as it turns out, virtually everything in life is simpler!

This final section of the book offers ideas for increasing your self-knowledge and awareness. These strategies, more than any others in the book, speak to the deeper aspects of your life. It's one thing to clear clutter from your junk drawer at the office, and another to clear your mind and become more of who you're meant to be.

90. Take action.

You'll never get to the treasure trove by staring at the treasure map. Planning is a good thing but not the only thing. Eventually, we all have to move out of the idea and planning stage and into the action stage.

The problem is often that we're too scared to take a step because we're not entirely certain of the path. We want to wait until we know the exact results of our actions before we make a move. So we stay stuck.

The solution is to take a step anyway. Even if you don't know the ultimate outcome of this journey, you can start moving forward.

A step based on your best guess is the right step to take. You have to *do*, in order to *be*. Even a simple life takes daily action steps.

91. Know your purpose.

You are here for a reason. Discovering that reason and using that knowledge as a beacon of light in your life is a fundamental step in a simpler, more fulfilled life.

Many problems and concerns will drop away once you're clear on your purpose.

When your life suits you, it becomes simpler.

92. Banish conformity.

To live a genuinely simple life, you're going to have to swim against the mainstream current. The status quo of our consumer society resists the ideology of simplicity. So we all have to ignore, to one extent or another, the pressures from outside to conform.

Simple living goes against the grain. Your intentions may be questioned; your plans may be sabotaged. You may often feel distracted from your commitment to a simple life by the overwhelming confusion of our society. As best as we can, those of us who choose a more simple way of being must ignore the myriad pressures to conform to others or to their ideas.

93. Ask not what others can do for you.

The only way to get what you want is to give it away. It's a great and mysterious paradox, and it's also a universal truth.

When you want more love, give more love. When you need more fulfillment, fulfill others. When you feel like you're running out of happiness, make someone else happy.

It's a major life-principle, and it's also useful as a life-strategy. When you're not sure what to do next, or where to turn, reach out and help someone. Give and your heart will be full.

94. Find your passion.

You've heard the clichés before: "Find your passion," "Follow your bliss," "Live your dream." However, there are truths in these sayings, that's why they became clichés! A life void of passionate endeavors is also empty of energy, balance and meaning.

When you see someone who is motivated, enthusiastic and just plain happy, you see an individual who has a passion. What's yours?

Find what excites *you*, what grabs your interest and holds you, what fills you up. Find it and follow it! It'll lead you to new horizons and to places and people you can't even imagine today.

You'll find the place where you belong and your special role there. No matter what your passion is, once you connect to it, your life will transform.

95. Be on mission.

Every successful business plan includes a mission statement—it's sound professional practice. What about on the personal side of things? How do you know you're on task if you don't know what that task is? How will you know when your mission is accomplished if you're vague about the mission? You're here for a reason; get to know why.

One survey respondent wrote that she uses her personal mission statement "to evaluate what actions I take, which invitations I accept and with whom I spend my time." Brilliant!

Abiding by your personal mission statement simplifies your life. You have an easier time making decisions because they're based on a solid foundation.

Each time you're faced with a decision about work, home, friends, events or any situation, you can compare your reaction or response with your mission statement. If one supports the other, you're good to go. If they clash, you can decide in a different direction.

96. Be yourself.

Be who you are. Sometimes, life advice can be that simple. When you get a handle on who you truly are and you move through the world with a strong sense of yourself, life is simplified without any further intervention.

Many responses in our survey revolved around this concept. Some suggestions were: Believe in yourself. Don't try to be anyone else. Do what you love to do. Follow your own road. Accept advice from others only when it fits with your set of values. Align your actions with what's in your heart.

And yet, being yourself can be one of the most challenging tasks you'll face. Why is it so hard to be our true self? Perhaps the answer lies in our desire to belong or to be accepted or to receive outside validation.

Whatever the reason, it's worth living your life from a solid position, grounded and centered in yourself. It can mean the difference between meaning and emptiness, between chaos and simplicity.

97. Practice gratitude.

Is your life filled with problems? If you spend much of your time and mental energy focusing on your problems, it's a sign that you don't practice gratitude.

Practicing gratitude means stepping out of the usual space of worry and problem-solving and into a space of being grateful for *what is*. You can pause your yearning for something other than what you've got and simply accept and embrace whatever it is that you currently have.

Just say "Yes" to what you have, especially the problems. This one strategy is so powerful that a daily habit of giving thanks (also known as counting your blessings) adds a whole new level of positive vibration to your life. It frees up much mental chatter, just to step back and be grateful for *something*—anything.

Whether it's for your good health, your best friend or for the view out of your window, there is always something to be grateful for. Most of, all give thanks and be grateful for all that you are.

98. Get clear on values.

Most of us have some idea of our value system. We learn much of it from our culture and community. But do you know precisely what you stand for? Apart from the status quo, what are *your* values? Do you stand for community and service? For freedom and democracy? For health and balance? For good humor? Positive thinking? Style? Art? Religion? Nature?

If you're not exactly certain of your value system, you may be drifting around in a choppy sea of imposed values and outside pressures that confuse and obscure your life. You can clear away a lot of doubt and disorder simply by knowing your values.

Drop values that don't belong to you. Align your life with your set of values. That's simplicity at its most pure.

99. Believe in yourself.

You really do have what it takes to live the life you want. Absolutely. You *can* make it happen. Your heart's desire is meant to be realized. You already have all the resources you need to begin. You deserve to be living your best life. You are worthy of the best. Do these statements resonate with you or do they make you uncomfortable? If you squirm when you're asked to appreciate your own innate worthiness, it may be time to take a deep look at your sense of self.

In your life, you will achieve precisely the measure of your self-worth. This means that whatever you have now, even the circumstances you don't like, is attributable to how worthy you believe you are. If you don't believe in yourself, truly, who will?

100. Remember, it's the journey, not the destination.

Even if a simpler life is your goal, it's still just a process. You can carefully select a set of the strategies for simplicity from this book and go about implementing them in your life. And even when you've finished, your life won't be "perfect." You won't be done building your best life. Because it's not "done" until you breathe your last breath.

Life, your life, is a journey. You're a traveler, finding and building your own path as you go, helping other travelers along the way. If your intention is clear, and you take positive action, then you'll create a better, simpler, easier, more enjoyable life.

101. Simplifying your life is an ongoing process.

Perhaps the simplest suggestion from our survey was: "Just be simple in whatever you do. Keep asking, 'Is this going to simplify my life?'"

Be simple: have a simple outlook, choose simple actions, make decisions based on which is the simplest; think simply and act simply.

Keep at it and continue to work towards making your life simpler and more satisfying.

"Sit down and have a good long think about what's important. Plan to rid yourself of the noose of long- and short-term debt and start living. You're a human doing, not just a human being, to quote someone from somewhere!"

—survey respondent

"The first step in simplifying your life is to figure out what makes you happy. I know to most that seems like a little easy thing to figure out, but too many people are chasing things that make others happy."

—survey respondent

"In today's complex and competitive world, we are now bombarded with all sorts of outside pressures, challenges, negative messages and what we think are "gotta do's." If you don't know your course, you can get stuck on this merry-go-round of trying to do it all but going nowhere and missing out on your true life path. When you know where you're going and what you stand for, you won't fall for anything and get stuck in the muck. In other words, learn to tell the unimportant, the negative, the time wasters and the naysayers to take a hike and get out of your way."

—survey respondent

Michael E. Angier

"Everyone thinks of changing the world, but no one thinks of changing himself."

—Leo Tolstoy, Russian mystic & novelist

Reports

101 Things I've Learned in My 50 Trips Around the Sun
www.SuccessNet.org/50trips

Books

Development First: Strategies for Self-Development by David B. Peterson, Mary Dee Hicks

Discover Your Empowering Purpose by Michael Angier

How to Create Your Vital Vision by Michael Angier

How to Create Your Meaningful Mission by Michael Angier

How to Uncover Your Compelling Core Values by Michael Angier

Programs, Courses & Other Resources

Your Core Values™ Online Course
Discover, define and begin living in accordance with your true values.
www.SuccessNet.org/go/ycv

A Thank You and a Request

Thank you for reading my book! I really appreciate all of your feedback, and I love hearing what you have to say.

I need your input to make the next version of this book—and my future books—better.

Please leave a brief and helpful review on Amazon to let me know what you thought of the book. Only about one in a thousand readers leave a review. I hope you will be a one-in-a-thousand reader.

You can use this link:
www.SuccessNet.org/go/amz-author

Thank you very much.

Michael E. Angier

BeYourBest@SuccessNet.org
www.SuccessNet.org

Mistakes Happen

We're committed to publishing inspiring, practical and professional books. However, mistakes do occur. If you should find a typographical, grammatical or factual error, we would be most grateful if you let us know. And, if you are the first to tell us about it, we'd be happy to send you a thank you gift.

Just email your find with the book name, location and type of error to BeYourBest@SuccessNet.org with "Found This!" in the subject. Thanks for your help.

About SuccessNet

SuccessNet is an international association of people committed to operating at their best—to creating excellence in every aspect of their lives and throughout their respective organizations. We support people in developing the skills, knowledge, belief and passion to achieve their dreams.

SuccessNet is dedicated to helping you become more knowledgeable, prosperous and effective.

Since 1995, over 200,000 people from all around the globe have benefited from the SuccessNet experience.

People from all walks of life become subscribers—small-business owners, managers and people who want to get ahead in their careers. Anyone who wants to maximize their potential, improve the quality of their lives and make a lasting difference in the world. SuccessNet is for great people who want to become even better.

Get a free subscription with your free report or book

Subscribe at www.SuccessNet.org

Success Networks International, Inc.
Tampa Bay, FL 34609-9546
Phone: 352.470-0812

About the Author

Michael E. Angier is the founder and CIO (Chief Inspiration Officer) of SuccessNet based in the Tampa Bay area of Florida. He's a father, grandfather, husband, writer, speaker, entrepreneur, coach and student.

He's the author of the *101 Best Ways series, The Achievement Code, The Secret to Being Fiercely Focused, How to Create a Vital Vision for Your Life, Discovering Your Empowering Purpose, How to Create Your Meaningful Mission, How to Uncover Your Compelling Core Values* and others.

Michael's work has been featured in numerous publications such as *USA Today, Selling Power, Personal Excellence* and *Sales & Marketing Excellence* as well as dozens of electronic publications. He's been interviewed on both TV and radio many times.

And his internationally popular articles have earned him a Paul Harris Fellowship with Rotary International.

Angier has experienced personal and professional success, but he's also suffered some bitter defeats. Although certainly preferring the former, he feels that he's learned the most from his struggles and disappointments. He feels that life's greatest lessons are learned by overcoming the obstacles in the path of a challenging and worthwhile objective.

Michael's passion is human potential. He believes fervently in the indomitable human spirit and revels in helping people and companies grow and prosper.

Over the past 40 years, Michael has devoted himself to studying what works and has been an ardent student of the principles of success. He's taught seminars and conducted workshops on goal setting, motivation and personal development in six countries.

Michael feels that there are three things essential to living a fulfilling and successful life: a purpose to live for, a self to live with and a faith to live by.

Michael is married to Dawn Angier—his partner, best friend, mentor, teacher, student and confidante. They have six adult children and several grandchildren. Michael enjoys tennis, reading, writing, publishing and helping people realize their dreams.

Other Books by Michael Angier

www.Amazon.com/author/michaelangier

The Achievement Code

The 3C Formula for Getting What You Truly Want

The Achievement Code offers a simple, but proven, formula for getting what you truly want. With the Three C's, the author has distilled down from both ancient and modern teachers the true alchemy of success and achievement.

Every single person who has ever achieved great things has employed the Three-C Formula. But not until Angier identified the Three Cs did the formula reveal itself. *The Achievement Code* outlines in simple, straightforward steps how to practice Clarity, Concentration and Consistency and actually get what you really want. Best-selling author, Bob Burg, says, "It contains the basic principles of success upon which Michael has built his own ultra-successful life and business and upon which anyone else can do the same. In these teachings, he lays the foundation from which anyone can decide on a certain goal and by the very nature of the instruction provided, go about achieving it. In fact, if one will follow all three of the "C's" he teaches us, I cannot see how it would be possible not to succeed."

How to Create Your Meaningful Mission

This Book is for You if You . . .

- want to maximize your time, energy and effort in a worthwhile cause— *your best life!*

- aren't satisfied with an average life—you want something bigger and better than that.

- want greater clarity for the path your life takes.

- desire to create a legacy—an exceptional life of meaning and significance—one that truly matters.

- are committed to creating a mission based upon your core values, strongly held beliefs and empowering purpose.

- desire to think bigger and believe in the possibilities of living up to your full and unique potential.

- want to believe more in yourself and in what's possible.

- want to learn about resources and recommendations that will help you create a clear and Meaningful Mission as a vehicle for living your Best Life.

- have a desire to dig deeper, think more comprehensively and live in a more balanced, meaningful and significant fashion.

-

Discover Your Empowering Purpose

Live Your Life with More Meaning, Significance and Fulfillment

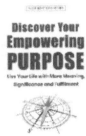

Mark Twain claimed, "The two most important days in your life are the day you're born and the day you find out why."

The existential question, "Why am I here?" does have an answer. You have an Empowering Purpose for your life. You only need to discover and uncover what it is.

This book helps you do that. And in doing so, you can live with more meaning, significance and fulfillment. You will have more confidence, exhibit more courage and have more commitment because you are fulfilling your purpose.

The author leads you by the hand as you determine your unique and special abilities and eventually your particular Zone of Genius.

Knowing and understanding your Empowering Purpose is a true game changer. If you're looking for more direction, inspiration, motivation, determination and devotion, read this book, go through the exercises and watch your life catch on fire.

The Secret to Being Fiercely Focused

How to Have More Energy, Less Stress and Get More Done by Tackling Your Tolerations

Are You Ready to Declutter Your Mind?

The Life-Changing Magic of Tidying Up: The Japanese Art of Decluttering and Organizing, has been off and on the New York Times Best Seller list for years— mostly on. If decluttering your home and office is life-changing, what about decluttering your *mind?*

Hundreds of thousands of books have been written on success—about what you need to get ahead. But what isn't talked about much is *what you need to get rid of.*

These niggly, spirit-sucking, energy-draining, peace-killers steal—often quite without detection—our joy, our happiness, our energy and our focus.

They are called Tolerations—things we tolerate, but shouldn't. And like weeds in a garden, we must recognize them for what they are and hoe them out—or they will take over our garden (life).

Do You Have a Clear Vision for Your Life?

How to Create a Vital Vision for Your Life gives you the impetus, the tools and the guidelines to create a meaningful, inspiring and detailed vision for your best life.

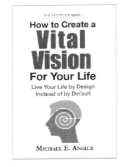

The author takes you by the hand and helps you dream big, think big and act even bigger.

This book will help you to . . .

- create a clear picture of the life you wish to create
- have more clarity and direction
- make better decisions and make them more easily
- have a bigger, better life
- have more balance in your life
- always know where you're going and what you want to achieve
- have more meaning and significance
- be more inspired, focused and motivated
- have more happiness by living on your terms

Don't let another day go by without creating a vivid and vital vision for your life. Get your copy of this book now and make the rest of your life the best of your life.

How to Uncover Your Compelling Core Values
Your Foundation for of a Truly Successful Life.

Your best life requires the uncovering of these values, getting clear on what they are and why they matter to you. Doing so will take you a long way toward your Empowering Purpose, your Meaningful Mission and your Vivid Vision.

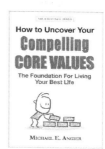

Without these Compelling Core Values, you are building on sand instead of bedrock. And that's a big reason for many failures.

This book takes you step by step through the core values process. It shows you exactly why this process is so valuable and then how to discover your top five core values, their hierarchy, and what they truly mean to you.

How to Uncover Your Compelling Core Values is based on SuccessNet's most popular online course which has helped thousands of people gain the clarity, perspective and confidence of living one's life with the integrity and conviction this process enables.

This book will help you make much better decisions. You will find yourself working on your highest priorities, getting more of the right things done with greater ease. If you want to live your best life—a more authentic, meaningful and significant life—this book is just what you need.

Free Resources

Best Life Self-Assessment

Download this free tool from SuccessNet. With it, you'll be able to evaluate yourself in many different areas of your life and find even more ideas for living your Empowering Purpose. Consider it your personal success inventory. www.SuccessNet.org/psa

Subscribe to SuccessNet.org at No Cost

If you would like to be part of SuccessNet, you can subscribe for free at www.SuccessNet.org

We offer a valuable gift like a book, special report or eCourse (it changes regularly) to anyone who joins our mailing list. And three to five times a month, you will receive an article from Michael on a topic in support of living your best life. And there are hundreds of articles, resources, recordings and more available on the website.

You can also follow SuccessNet on Facebook at www.Facebook.com/ILikeSuccessNet or Michael's personal page at www.Facebook.com/michaelangier

Dedication

This book is dedicated to my six children. Although they didn't necessarily *simplify* my life, they did enrich it beyond all measure.

Michael, Michelle, Sarah, Bradford, Kevin and William are people who are, or soon will be, making a lasting difference in the world. They are definitely people who care about things that matter. And each of them brings something unique to my life and the lives of those they touch.

I love them, I'm proud of them, and I think about them every day.

May they, and the children they have, find ideas in this book that will allow them to live more simply in an often complicated world.

I'm grateful for what they have taught me and what they continue to teach me.

Acknowledgements

"101 Great Ideas to Simplify Your Life" started as a survey of the nearly 100,000 valued members and subscribers of SuccessNet. We asked them for their best ideas for ways to simplify our lives. We are sincerely grateful for their contribution.

From there, Sarah Pond worked over many weeks sorting, filtering, organizing and summarizing the many candidates for the top 101 great ideas. Sarah's talent, hard work and dedication are most appreciated.

I'm blessed to be married to the smartest woman I know. In addition, she's beautiful, hard-working and fun. The editing and proofing fell to her, and she shined as she always does. Thank you, Dawn.

My mastermind partners and many of my colleagues reviewed and critiqued the manuscript, provided much needed support, and wrote their praises. And for that I am truly grateful.

And last, but certainly not least, I acknowledge you, the reader of this book for wanting to simplify your life, so as to enjoy more serenity and fulfillment.

—Michael Angier

72249606R00066